Magic Moments™
Amazing Math With Your Kids

Written by Patricia A. Staino
Illustrated by Marilynn G. Barr

The Education Center, Inc.
Greensboro, North Carolina

For my math teachers. . .
You truly earned it!

ISBN# 1-56234-175-8

Cover design by Clevell Harris
Cover illustration by Lois Axeman

The Education Center, Inc.
Box 9753
Greensboro, NC 27429-0753

Manufactured in the United States
10 9 8 7 6 5 4 3 2 1

AMAZING MATH

WITH YOUR KIDS

Table of Contents

Table of Contents

Dear Kids,

You may not like math very much. You may think all the numbers are confusing and all the facts are hard to remember.

Or maybe you LOVE math. Maybe you enjoy figuring out how to add, subtract, multiply, and divide.

No matter how much you like or don't like math, this book will make you love it! That's because it's not filled with a long list of problems that you need to figure out. In this book, you'll find lots of games, puzzles, stories, and projects that make math easy and fun!

And you don't need a lot of stuff to do each activity. Find a deck of playing cards, a pair of dice, some pencils, and paper, and you'll have most of what you need for the games in this book.

You'll use math a lot as you get older. You probably use it a lot now. You use math when you count up your allowance or add up the coins in your piggy bank. You use math when you count the change in your pocket to see if you have enough money to buy ice cream. You use math when you bake brownies. You even use math to play some sports!

So pull out your pencils and grab a grown-up friend. It's time to get counting and have some fun.

Dear Parents,

If your child's teacher told you to help your child practice math, you might wonder how to do that without making you both fill your weekends with homework.

Or if the teacher told you to help your child develop his or her already excellent math skills, you may wonder how to offer your child something new.

No matter what the situation, this book is a great way to start. It's filled with games and puzzles and projects that will entertain your child and still be fun for you. Your child won't even realize he is practicing math. Many of the activities are games of chance and strategy and will be just as challenging for you as for your child.

Some of the games may seem similar—there are a few versions of both bingo and tic-tac-toe, for example. That's because children learn with repetition. However, each version of a game is a bit different, developing a different math skill or thinking strategy. So try them all— one is bound to become a favorite.

Maybe math was never your favorite subject. Maybe you still cringe when you have to figure out percentages. But this is not the same old math textbook. This collection of games will put a smile on your face and provide hours of fun with your child.

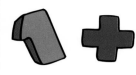 + # About This Book

Before you get started, read this page to learn a little about what you'll find in this book.

Calculator Ratings

On the top of each activity page, there is a calculator rating. You will see either one, two, three, or four calculators. They tell you if a game is easy or hard. Activities with one calculator are the easiest, and those with four are the most challenging.

If you find an activity that sounds fun but is rated easier or more difficult than you would like, try it anyway and see what you can learn.

Adding It All Up

The "Adding It Up" pages are chock-full of special information. You can learn how other people write their numbers and the special meanings of certain numbers. You'll learn how counting was invented and how to make an ancient counting machine. You'll learn about different kinds of clocks and how people started using money. Amuse your friends with all the new bits of information that you learn! And don't forget to try the activity ideas in the "Try this" boxes on each "Adding It Up" page. These special projects will give you new and nifty number experiences.

ArithmeTRICKs and Math Giggles

Share your math smarts with your friends. Try the "ArithmeTRICK" puzzles on your friends and amaze them with your mathematical genius. And the "Math Giggles" are just little jokes and riddles to help you see how much fun math can be.

Stop Signs

STOP This symbol means you need a grown-up to help you with this step.

Recognizing Numbers

How many different ways can you show the number five?
Five. 5. /////. V. These are all symbols for the number five. There
are many ways to say and show numbers, but the *value* of the
number is still the same. If you want to have fun with math and
learn lots of math games and tricks and puzzles, you must first
learn how to tell one number from the other.

Adding It Up—Other Numbers

The numbers we use today are based on the Arabic numbers. Look at the chart below to see how the numbers changed over 1,000 years.

1	2	3	4	4	6	7	8	9	
1	2	3	8	4	6	ʌ	8	9	0
1	2	3	4	5	6	7	8	9	0
1	2	3	4	5	6	7	8	9	10

1,000 years ago
800 years ago
600 years ago
today

Everyone doesn't write numbers the same way we do. Take a look at these different number systems.

EGYPTIAN

1	2	3	4	5	6	7	8	9	10	100	1,000

HINDU-ARABIC

0	1	2	3	4	5	6	7	8	9	10

ANCIENT GREEK

1	2	3	4	5	6	7	8	9	10
A	B	Γ	Δ	E	F	Z	H	θ	I

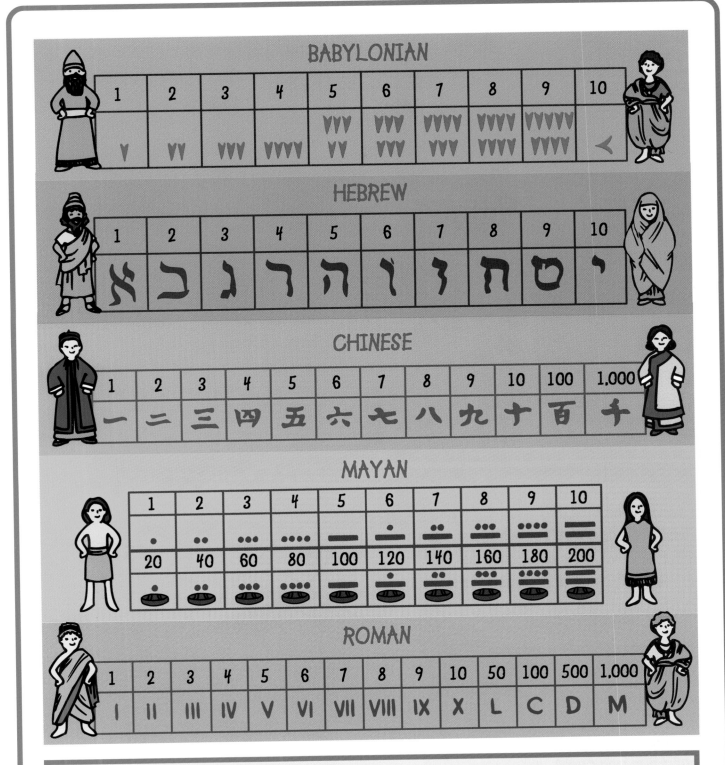

BABYLONIAN

	1	2	3	4	5	6	7	8	9	10

HEBREW

	1	2	3	4	5	6	7	8	9	10
	א	ב	ג	ד	ה	ו	ז	ח	ט	י

CHINESE

	1	2	3	4	5	6	7	8	9	10	100	1,000
	一	二	三	四	五	六	七	八	九	十	百	千

MAYAN

	1	2	3	4	5	6	7	8	9	10
	20	40	60	80	100	120	140	160	180	200

ROMAN

	1	2	3	4	5	6	7	8	9	10	50	100	500	1,000
	I	II	III	IV	V	VI	VII	VIII	IX	X	L	C	D	M

Try this:

- Make up your own system. Can you think of a new way to write numbers? Write out the numbers 1 through 20, 50, 100, and 1000.
- Try writing out some different math problems using one of the other writing systems.

Leaping Lizards

2 or more players
Learn your numbers with the help of some creepy-crawly creatures.

You'll need:
2 hinged clothespins
construction paper
scissors
glue
black marker
yardstick
18-inch by 24-inch sheet of brown
    paper or piece of cardboard
2 small beanbags or some other kind of
    small marker that can be thrown

4. The first player throws his beanbag onto the number board. He moves his lizard that many numbers on the yardstick. For example, if the first player lands on a 4, he moves his lizard to the number 4 on the yardstick. If he lands on 2 the next time he throws his beanbag, he moves his lizard to the number 6. The first player to get to the end of the stick wins.

1. Decorate the clothespins to look like lizards. Use construction paper, scissors, and glue to make tails like the one below. Draw eyes and teeth on the ends that open and close. (Make each lizard a different color.)

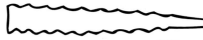

2. Divide the cardboard into 12 equal squares, as shown here. Write in the numbers 1, 2, 3, and 4, in any order.

1	4	3	1
3	2	1	4
2	4	3	1

← 24 inches →   18 inches

3. Give one beanbag and one lizard to each player. Place the yardstick on a table where everyone can see it.

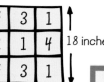

For a more advanced game:
Each player gets two beanbags. Throw both bean bags onto the square, one at a time. Add those two numbers together. If you answer correctly, you move that many numbers on the yardstick. If you answer incorrectly, you stay where you are.

Pick 'Em Up Quick

3 or more players

Are you the fastest number picker in the land?

You'll need:
12 index cards for the caller
4 index cards for each player
black marker

1. Write the numbers 2, 3, 4, and 5, each on its own index card. Do this for each player in the game.

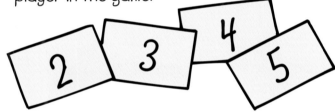

2. Draw two, three, four, or five dots on each of the caller's index cards. Make three cards for each number of dots. Arrange the dots any way you like (see below for some ideas).

3. Ask the caller to shuffle the dot cards and place them in a pile on the table. The other players arrange their numbered index cards in front of themselves.

4. The caller draws the first card from the deck. She holds up the card so everyone playing can see it.

caller

5. The players quickly pick up the number card that matches the number of dots on the caller's card. The first player to hold up the matching card gets a point. When all the caller's cards have been drawn, the player with the most points wins.

13

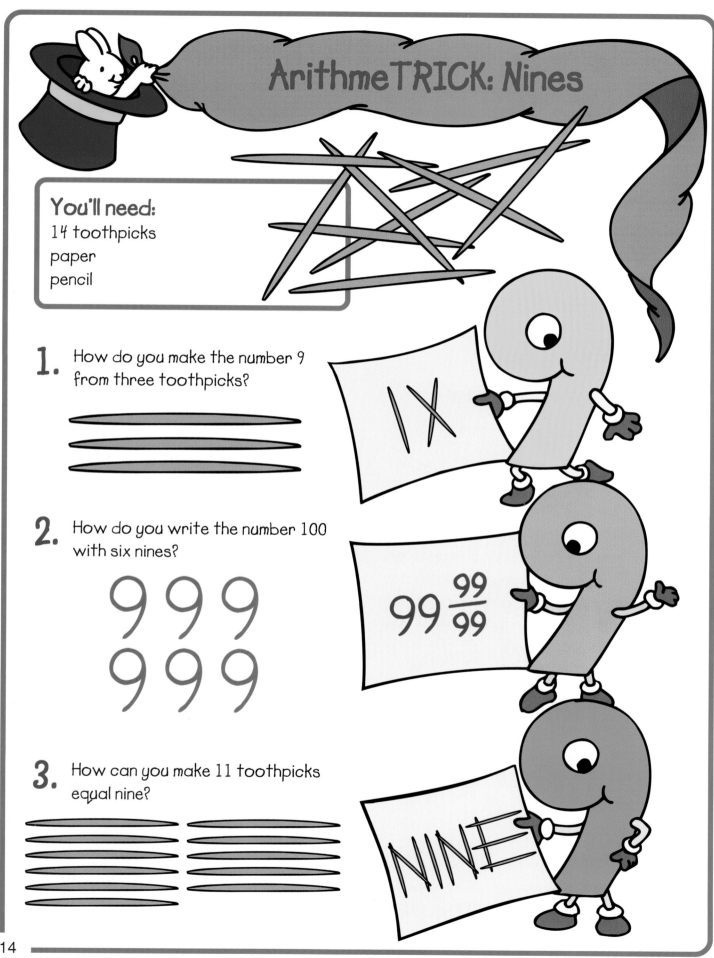

ArithmeTRICK: Nines

You'll need:
14 toothpicks
paper
pencil

1. How do you make the number 9 from three toothpicks?

2. How do you write the number 100 with six nines?

$$999$$
$$999$$

3. How can you make 11 toothpicks equal nine?

Mini Bingo

2 players

This quick version of bingo makes learning your numbers easy.

You'll need:

four 8½-inch by 11-inch sheets of construction paper or pieces of cardboard

black marker

small plastic bag

pencil

scissors

1. On one piece of construction paper draw the graph below. *Number the boxes from 1 to 8.* On another piece of construction paper, draw the same graph. *Number those boxes from 9 to 16.* The numbers in the boxes should be out of order.

2. On another piece of construction paper, draw 16 circles, like the one below. *Number the circles from 1 to 16.* (STOP) Cut them out and put them in the plastic bag.

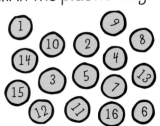

3. On the last piece of construction paper, draw 16 more circles. (STOP) Cut them out. Give eight to each player.

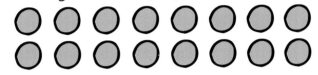

4. To play the game, you take turns closing your eyes and drawing one of the numbered circles out of the bag. Call out the number. If you have that number on your card, place one of your blank circles on top of it. The winner is the first person to get four circles in a row.

To make the game easier or harder, change the number of squares on the bingo card.

15

Adding It Up—Legends of Numbers

When we think of numbers, we just think of how they help us count or how they tell us how many things there are. But ancient people believed many things about numbers. Here is some of the history and legend surrounding some favorite numbers.

Zero
Zero stands for nothing. We need zero to hold empty places. Without zeros, 100 becomes 1. And that is just not the same thing. The Maya Indians invented the idea of zero around the fourth century. The symbol "0" began in India around the ninth century.

One
The ancient Greeks believed that one was the only real, true number. That's because ones make up all the other numbers. The Greeks thought one was so important, they made it their symbol for thought.

Two
Two is the first number that can be broken up into two separate, equal parts. Long ago, the number two would represent opposite things—night and day, sky and earth, boy and girl. In fact, in ancient China and Greece, two was thought of as a *girl* number (along with all even numbers).

Three
The ancient Greeks thought three was the first odd number (rather than one) because it cannot be broken up equally. They thought of three and other odd numbers as *boy* numbers. People that lived long ago thought three was a little bit magical. That's because many important things came in threes, like the animal, vegetable, and mineral kingdoms of the earth.

Four
The Greeks thought of the number four as the number of law and justice, because it could be divided into two equal (fair) parts.

Five
The Greeks believed five was the number of marriage. That's because it is made up of 2 and 3, which are the first girl and boy numbers.

 ## Six

The Greeks called six the "perfect" number. They discovered that the number can be evenly divided by one, two, and three, and that those three numbers add up to six. The number six represented life and good luck.

Seven

Seven is still thought to be lucky today, but in ancient times it was considered magical because the moon changed shape every seven days.

 ## Eight

Eight has meant many things to many people. The Greeks thought it stood for wisdom. The ancient Hindus believed the world was made up of eight parts. And the ancient Chinese counted eight seasons in their year.

Nine

Nine is thought of as a symbol of truth because of the strange ways it behaves. Most number that can be equally divided by nine will also be made up of two digits that equal nine or are a multiple of nine when they are added together (2 x 9 = 18, 1 + 8 = 9).

 ## Ten

In the ancient world, many people thought of ten as a new beginning. And in the way we count, it still is. When we reach ten, we start over at one: 8, 9, 10, 11, 12, etc. The word *eleven* means "ten and one left over," *twelve* means "ten and two left over," and so on down the line. This is so because when people learned to count they used their fingers, and there are only ten of those to count.

Try this:
- Draw pictures to represent each number. Pretend you are an ancient Greek. How will you draw each number?

Milk Cap Match

2 players
Try this speedy game of matching for big fun.

You'll need:
20 milk jug caps
2 sheets of construction paper
2 plastic bags
glue
variety of 60 very small objects, such
    as buttons, unpopped popcorn
    kernels, and beans
black marker
scissors

1. On one sheet of construction paper, trace ten milk caps. **STOP** Cut them out. Do this again with the other sheet of construc-tion paper. Number four circles with the number 1, four with 2, four with 3, four with 4, and four with 5. Put two of each number in each plastic bag.

2. Next, make one set of milk jug caps—glue one small object on the first cap, two small objects on the second cap, three small objects on the third cap, four small objects on the fourth cap, and five small objects on the fifth cap. Now make three more sets in the same way.

3. Put two sets of caps in one plastic bag, and two sets in the other.

4. Shake up both plastic bags. Each player gets one bag. One player yells go, and you both empty your bags out onto a table or floor. Match each numbered circle to a milk cap with that number of objects. The first player to match all his circles and caps is the winner.

ArithmeTRICK: All Roads Lead to 99

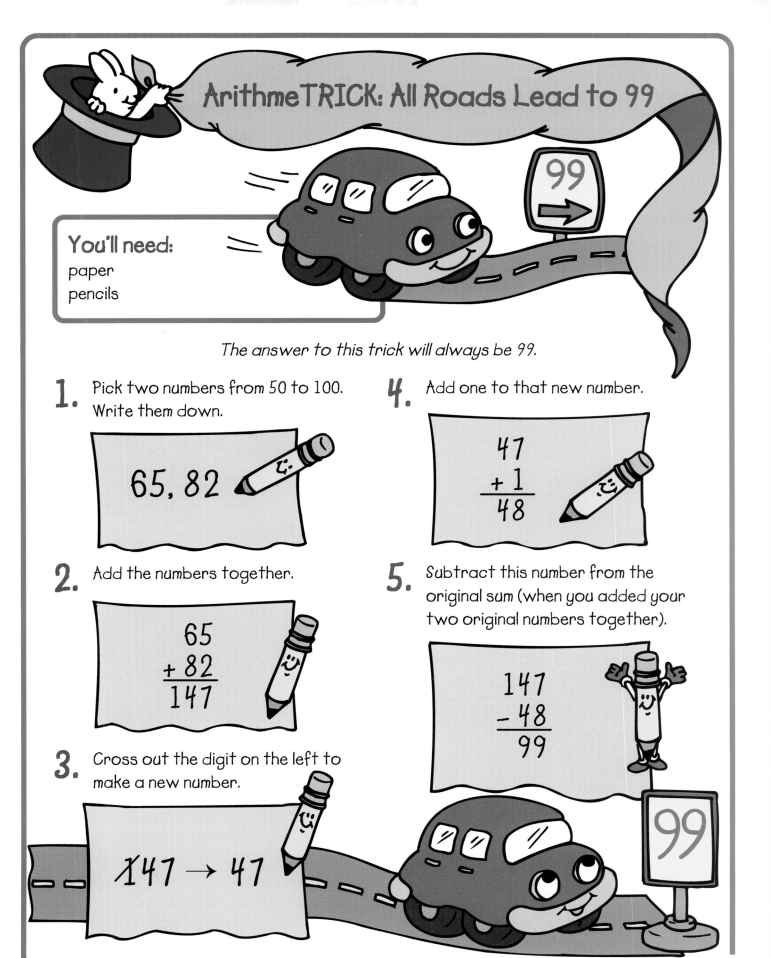

You'll need:
paper
pencils

The answer to this trick will always be 99.

1. Pick two numbers from 50 to 100. Write them down.

65, 82

2. Add the numbers together.

$$\begin{array}{r} 65 \\ + 82 \\ \hline 147 \end{array}$$

3. Cross out the digit on the left to make a new number.

147 → 47

4. Add one to that new number.

$$\begin{array}{r} 47 \\ + 1 \\ \hline 48 \end{array}$$

5. Subtract this number from the original sum (when you added your two original numbers together).

$$\begin{array}{r} 147 \\ - 48 \\ \hline 99 \end{array}$$

Color Kid

2 or more players
Who will be the first to color in her Kid?

You'll need:
1 piece of tracing paper for each player
1 pencil for each player
pair of dice
crayons

1. Each player traces the Kid on the next page.

2. Roll the dice. Color the part of your Kid that matches the number you rolled. You may color either the combined number, or each number on each die. For example, if you roll a "2" and a "6," you color sections "2" and "6," or just section "8." Each player takes a turn rolling the dice. If you roll numbers that you have already colored in, you do nothing, and the next person rolls.

3. The winner is the first person to color all the sections of her Kid.

or

Math Giggles
Q: What Roman numeral grows?
A: The numeral for four—IV (ivy).

20

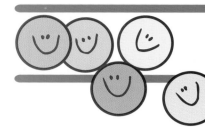

Math Memory Game

2 players

To win this game you need to know your numbers and remember where they are.

You'll need:
20 index cards
black marker

1. Write the word "one" on an index card. Write the number "1" on another card. On a third card, draw one dot. On a fourth card, draw one smiley face. Do this with the rest of the cards for the numbers 2 through 5 (for example, write "two" and "2," draw two dots, and draw two smiley faces).

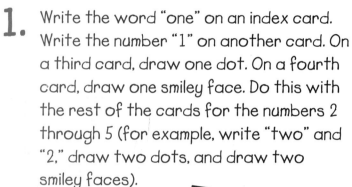

2. Shuffle the cards to mix them up. Spread them out on a tabletop, so the blank sides are facing up.

3. To start the game, turn over one card. Then turn over another card. If both cards match, take both cards. Now go again. As long as you get a match, you keep going. If they don't match, turn the cards over so they face down. Then it's the next player's turn. (Two cards match if they are versions of the same number. For example, the "two" card and the card with two dots match. But five smiley faces and one smiley face do NOT match.)

4. The game is over when all the cards are gone. The player with the most cards wins.

Math Giggles
Q: If 300 sheep, 3 shepherds, 2 horses, and 3 dogs were all in a field together, how many feet could you count?
A: Six feet. The rest are paws and hooves.

Number Sequence & Value

A number's value depends on where it is located. Sometimes it is in the ones column, sometimes in the tens column, sometimes in the hundreds column, and so on. The games and activities in this section will help you remember which column means what.

Lucky 7

2 or more players

Is it luck or skill that makes the winner in this game?

You'll need:
40 index cards
black marker
1 die

1. With a grown-up's help, write a number with one 7 in it on each of the index cards. Write some small numbers, with one or two digits, and write some larger numbers, up to seven digits.

271   7,432,186

2. On the back of each card, write the *place value* of the 7 in that number. For example, if the number on the front is 72, you write *tens* on the back. If the number on the front is 7,345, your write *thousands* on the back.

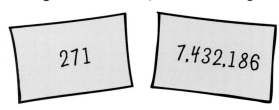

271 → tens   7,432,186 → millions

3. Now you're ready to play. Shuffle the cards and stack them so the numbered sides are facing up. Roll the die. If you roll a 6, you lose your turn. If you roll a 1, 2, 3, 4, or 5, you pick that many cards from the top of the pile.

4. Read the number on each card and tell the other players the place value of the 7 in that number. Keep the cards for the values you get right. If you get any wrong, put those cards at the bottom of the stack in the center of the table.

5. The game is over when there are no cards left. The player with the most cards in his own stack is the lucky winner.

tens

24

ArithmeTRICK: Read My Mind

You'll need:

pencils

paper

With this trick, your friends will think you can read their minds.

Tell your friend to do the following steps:

1. Write any two numbers from 1 through 9.

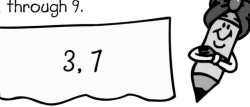

$$3, 7$$

2. Multiply one of the numbers by 5.

$$\begin{array}{r} 3 \\ \times 5 \\ \hline 15 \end{array}$$

3. Add 3 to that answer.

$$\begin{array}{r} 15 \\ + 3 \\ \hline 18 \end{array}$$

4. Double that answer.

$$\begin{array}{r} 18 \\ + 18 \\ \hline 36 \end{array}$$

5. Add the other number you chose (in step 1) to that answer.

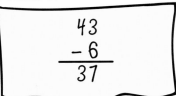

$$\begin{array}{r} 36 \\ + 7 \\ \hline 43 \end{array}$$

6. Ask your friend what answer she got. In your head subtract 6 from that number.

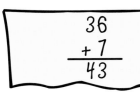

$$\begin{array}{r} 43 \\ - 6 \\ \hline 37 \end{array}$$

7. The digits in the answer are the two original numbers.

The original numbers are 3 and 7.

Big & Small

2 or more players
Can you earn 150 points before everyone else?

You'll need:
1 pencil for each player
2 sheets of paper for each player
1 pair of dice

1. Roll the dice. Look at the two numbers you roll. Write down the biggest number you can make from those digits. (For example, if you roll a 3 and a 4, the biggest number is 43. If you roll a 1 and a 6, the biggest number you can make is 61.)

2. Roll the dice again. Write down the smallest number you can make from the two numbers you roll this time. (For example, if you roll a 1 and a 4, the smallest number is 14. If you roll a 2 and a 5, the smallest number is 25.)

3. Subtract the small number from the large number. (If the second number is not small enough to subtract from the first number, roll again.) That is your score. Write it down on your second piece of paper.

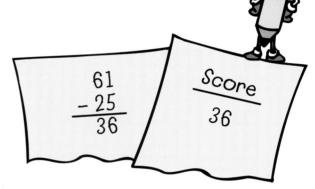

4. Each player takes his turn rolling the dice. The second time you take a turn, you add that score to the first score. The third time you take a turn, you add that score to the sum of the first two scores, and so on.

5. The winner is the first player to reach 150 points.

For a more challenging game, try using three dice.

Take a Spin

2 to 6 players

Can you you guess where the spinner will land?

You'll need:

pencils

paper

spinner from a board game
with the numbers 0 through 9*

1. Each player gets a piece of paper and a pencil.

2. Everyone draws three blanks on his or her paper.

3. Spin the spinner. Each player writes that number on one of the blanks. After three spins, when all the blanks are filled, everyone reads out the numbers. The player with the largest number wins the round and gets a point. The first player who gets a score of 10 wins the game.

Other ways to play: See who can write down the smallest number or try using four or five blanks.

*If you do not have a spinner, use playing cards. Use the numbered cards and the aces, and have the ace count as 1 and the 10 count as 0.

Math Giggles

Q: If you see 20 dogs running down the street, what time is it?

A: Nineteen after one.

27

Adding It Up—What's a Googol?

A googol sounds like a furry monster or a dessert from another country, but it's really a number! It's a really BIG number.

A *googol* is a 1 with 100 zeros after it! How long do you think it would take you to write that number?

The name was invented in the early 1900s by a mathematician named Edward Kasner. Actually, it was invented by his 9-year-old nephew, Milton Sirotta. Mr. Kasner was thinking up names for really big numbers, and he asked Milton for a suggestion. Milton came up with googol, which he liked because it sounded like silly baby talk. It *is* kind of funny to think of serious mathematicians talking about googols!

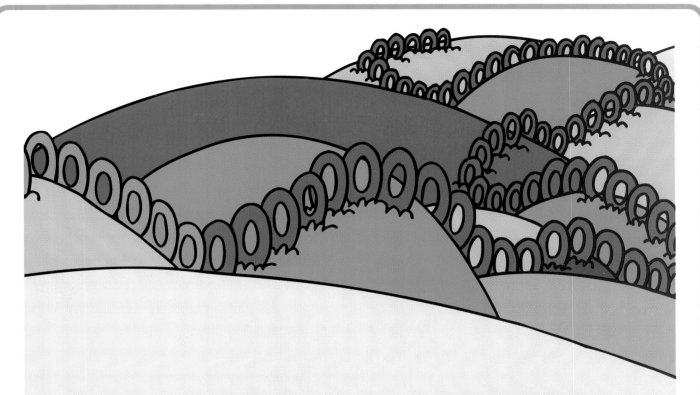

But a googol isn't the biggest number. There is a *googolplex*, which is a 1 followed by 10,000 zeros! But even that isn't the biggest number. You can add as many zeros as you want to any number, and it still wouldn't be the biggest number. If you add 1 to the biggest number you can think of, you are making an even bigger number.

Numbers are infinite. That means they go on forever. You can always think of an even bigger number because you can always add 1 to any number.

Today, the words googol and googolplex are used by mathematicians all over the world, including China, Russia, Europe, and Israel.

Try this:
- Try writing out a googol. How long does it take? How much paper do you need?
- Once you know how long it would take to write out a googol, try to figure out how long it would take to write out a googolplex.
- Think of some interesting names for some really big numbers.

Pirates' Treasure Hunt

2 to 4 players

Which pirate will bring home the biggest booty bag?

You'll need:

large piece of cardboard or poster board
construction paper, cut into
    forty 3-inch by 1-inch pieces
1 marker
40 play coins, tokens, disks, or
    small cardboard circles

3. Shuffle the numbered cards and place them in a stack, facedown, in the center of the board. Put the play coins on top of the treasure chest. Each player chooses one side of the board to be his "treasure chest."

4. To play, draw a card from the stack. Place the card on the 1000, 100, 10, or 1 space on your side of the board. Players take turn drawing cards until all the spaces are filled. The player who makes the biggest number wins the round and gets one coin to place on his booty bag space. For the next round place all the cards back in the deck and shuffle them. The first player to get ten coins wins the game.

1. Write each number 0 through 9 on four different pieces of paper.

2. Ask a grown-up to draw the board on the next page on the poster board. (Your helper can trace the treasure chest below, if he needs to.)

Ten To Win!

	1	10	100	1000	
1					1
10					10
100					100
1000					1000
	1000	100	10	1	

31

Art by Number

Make a beautiful collage out of your favorite number.

You'll need:

old magazines
scissors
glue
one 12-inch by 18-inch
    piece of paper
pencil
colored marker

1. Pick your favorite number. Write that number in the center of the paper, and make it big.

> 7

2. Page through the magazines and find pictures you like. (STOP) With a grown-up's help, cut them out. You need the same number of pictures as the number you wrote on the paper. So if you wrote 9, you need to cut out nine pictures that will fit on the paper. Count the pictures out loud as you cut them out of the magazines.

3. When you have all your pictures, count them again to be sure you have the right number. Now paste them to the paper, in any design you like. Count each picture as you glue it down.

4. When you've glued all the pictures to the paper, count them all again to be sure you have the right number. Then number each picture from 1 through whichever number you chose.

For a real challenge, look for pictures that show the same number of items as the number you chose. For example, if you chose 3, you would find three pictures of three things each, like three eggs, three babies, and three flowers.

ArithmeTRICK: More Mind Reading Math

You'll need:

pencils

paper

The answer to this puzzle will always be 60.

Ask a friend to do the following steps:

1. Choose a number from 1 through 100.

2. Add 10 to that number.

3. Double that answer.

4. Add 100 to that answer.

5. Take half that answer.

6. Subtract the original number from that answer.

7. Tell your friend you can read his mind: the answer is 60.

1.   50

2.   50
     + 10
       60

3.   60
     + 60
      120

4.   120
     + 100
       220

5.   110
     2)220
        2
        2
        2
        0

6.   110
     − 50
       60

60?!

Roll 'Em Up

2 to 6 players

You can lose this game if you earn too many points.

You'll need:
1 pencil for each player
1 sheet of paper for each player
1 die

1. Each player should make a score sheet like the one below.

Tens	Ones
1.	
2.	
3.	
4.	
5.	
6.	
7.	

2. Take turns rolling the die. When you roll, write that number in either the left or right column. Write a 0 in the other column.

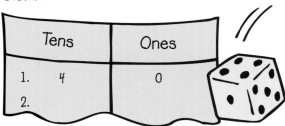

Tens	Ones
1. 4	0
2.	

3. After everyone has rolled the die seven times, add up your columns.

4. The player who comes closest to 100 without going over is the winner.

Tens	Ones
1. 4	0
2. 0	3
3. 0	2
4. 3	0
5. 2	0
6. 0	1
7. 0	3
9	6

Bowlful of Marbles

2 players

Can you pick up roly-poly marbles with chopsticks?

You'll need:
large bowl
2 medium-size paper cups
50 different-sized marbles
4 chopsticks

1. Place the marbles in the bowl.

2. Take turns trying to pick up as many marbles as you can with the chopsticks. You may use only one hand to control the chopsticks.

3. You must lift the marble or marbles from the bowl to your paper cup. If you lift a marble and it drops at any time before you get it in your cup, your turn is over.

4. The game is over when all the marbles are gone. Look at the two cups. Can you guess who has the most marbles?

5. Now take turns counting your marbles out loud. The player with the most marbles wins.

Patterns

Patterns are all around you. A pattern is when things repeat themselves in a regular way. If you sit boy/girl/boy/girl in school, that's a pattern. If you emptied out a bag of M&M's® on a tabletop and lined them up so there was a green one, a red one, a yellow one, a green one, a red one, and a yellow one, that would be a pattern. Understanding patterns can help you understand numbers and math.

Snowflakes

*Snowflakes are an example of symmetry,
a kind of pattern in a single object.*

You'll need:

white paper
drawing compass
pencil
scissors

1. **STOP** Ask a grown-up to help you use the compass to draw a circle on the paper.

2. **STOP** Cut out the circle. Fold the circle in half. Fold it in half again. *

Fold.   Fold.
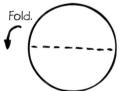

3. **STOP** Carefully cut designs into the paper. Unfold your snowflake when you are finished. What do you notice about your snowflake? You'll see that both sides are exactly the same. Also, if you make more than one, you will see that all your paper flakes come out different, just like real snowflakes!

4. Tape your snowflakes to the window, hang them from the ceiling, or make a mobile out of them.

*Try folding the circle a third and fourth time. How does your snowflake look now?

Chart Patterns

What kind of patterns can you find in a certain group of numbers?

You'll need:

large piece of poster
    board or cardboard
black marker
ruler
dried beans

1. Ask a grown-up to help you make a chart like the one on the next page, using the poster board, marker, and ruler.

2. Use the beans to cover different patterns of numbers. Try:

   • Numbers with a 5 in them
   • Numbers with a 2 in them
   • Numbers with a 0 in them
   • Numbers with a 1 in them
   • Multiples of 4
   • Numbers that you can evenly divide by 3
   • Numbers with two even digits
   • Numbers where one digit is half of the other (like 42, 36, etc.)

3. Do the numbers make sensible patterns? What other patterns can you make?

4. Try making smaller charts, with five columns across and five rows down, eight columns across and eight columns down, etc. Also, find out if the charts work if there are not the same number of columns and rows. Try making a chart with four columns across and five rows down, or six columns across and four rows down.

Numbers that are even.

0	1		3		5		7		9
	11		13	14	15	16	17	18	19
20	21	22	23	24	25	26	27	28	29
30	31	32	33	34	35	36	37	38	39
40	41	42	43	44	45	46	47	48	49
50	51	52	53	54	55	56	57	58	59
60	61	62	63	64	65	66	67	68	69
70	71	72	73	74	75	76	77	78	79
80	81	82	83	84	85	86	87	88	89
90	91	92	93	94	95	96	97	98	99

0	1	2	3	4	5	6	7	8	9
10	11	12	13	14	15	16	17	18	19
20	21	22	23	24	25	26	27	28	29
30	31	32	33	34	35	36	37	38	39
40	41	42	43	44	45	46	47	48	49
50	51	52	53	54	55	56	57	58	59
60	61	62	63	64	65	66	67	68	69
70	71	72	73	74	75	76	77	78	79
80	81	82	83	84	85	86	87	88	89
90	91	92	93	94	95	96	97	98	99

Fruit Kabobs

*Make fancy patterns when
you make good stuff to eat!*

You'll need:
plastic knife
assorted fruits such as orange, apple,
    and pear slices, grapes, and bananas
wooden skewers

1. **STOP** With a grown-up's help, cut the fruit into chunks.

2. Make some fruit kabobs, each with a different pattern.
Try:
    grape, orange, grape, orange,
        grape, orange
    apple, pear, banana, apple, pear,
        banana, apple, pear
    grape, apple, orange, apple, grape

3. Can you explain what a pattern is after studying your kabobs? What other patterns can you make with the fruit?

4. When you're finished, snack on your kabobs!

Basket O' Beans

2 players

Be the first player to collect three matching beans.

You'll need:

bowl of 4 different kinds of dried
    beans (black, kidney, lima, pinto)
2 plastic bowls
5-inch square piece of cardboard
spinner arrow
black marker
paper fastener
glue

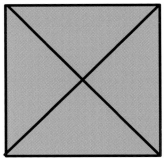

1. Ask a grown-up to help you make the spinner. With the marker, divide the cardboard into four sections like the one shown below.

2. Glue one different bean in each section.

3. Poke a small hole in the middle of the cardboard. Attach the arrow to the cardboard with the paper fastener. When the glue has dried you are ready to play.

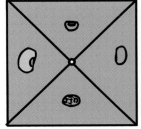 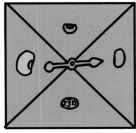

4. Take turns spinning the arrow. When you land on a bean, take one of that kind of bean out of the bowl and place it in your plastic bowl.

5. The first player to collect three of the same kind of bean is the winner.

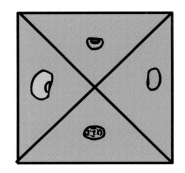

ArithmeTRICK: Toothpick Magic

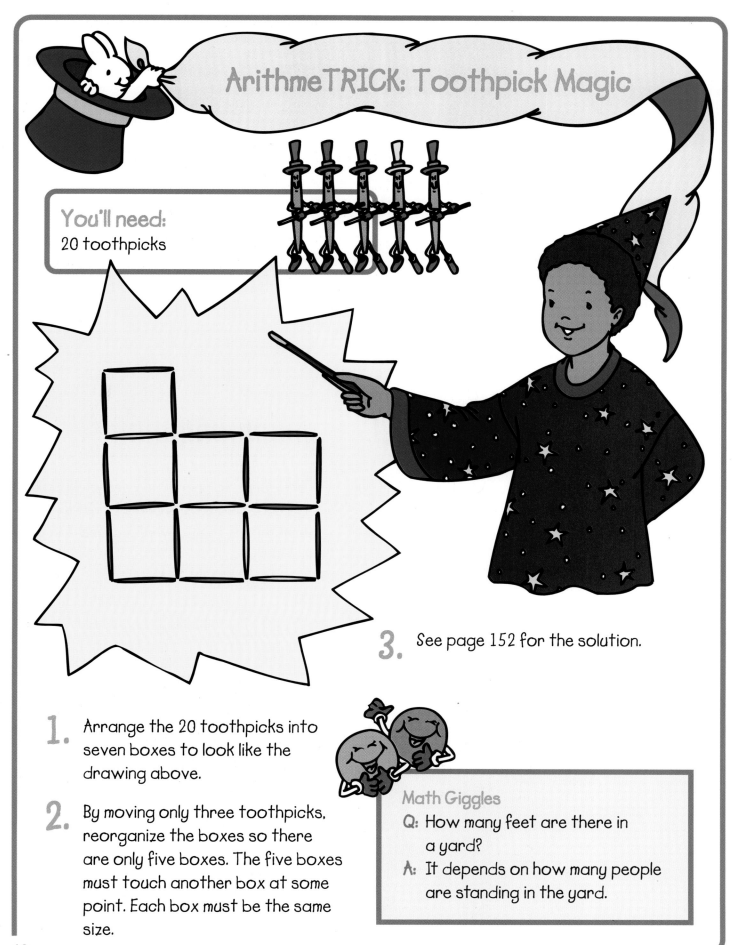

You'll need:
20 toothpicks

3. See page 152 for the solution.

1. Arrange the 20 toothpicks into seven boxes to look like the drawing above.

2. By moving only three toothpicks, reorganize the boxes so there are only five boxes. The five boxes must touch another box at some point. Each box must be the same size.

Math Giggles
Q: How many feet are there in a yard?
A: It depends on how many people are standing in the yard.

Counting

Lots of people count every day. Math teachers count, you know that. But so do astronauts, poets, bankers, clothing designers, post office workers, race car drivers, nurses, and many other workers. Everyone needs to know how to tell how many "things" they need or have or must do. You can count on it!

Adding It Up—The Abacus

The abacus was the first calculator. These counting machines were invented about 5,000 years ago, in Egypt, Babylon, and China. In those days, lots of merchants were trading back and forth. They traded grain, gems, wine, silk, and many other things. But they needed to keep track of how much they bought and sold. They needed a way other than their hands to add and subtract numbers.

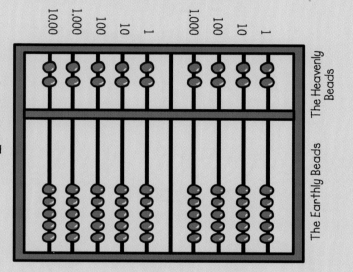

Sometimes when you buy something at the store, you say you are going to the "counter" to pay for it. That's because long ago, a store owner would sit at a table with his counter, or abacus, waiting for customers to pay. Many shopkeepers in Asian countries still use an abacus today.

The word abacus comes from a word in ancient times that meant "dust" or "sand."

In Babylon, they would draw lines in the sand. The first line would be the ones column. The second line to the left would be the tens column, and so on.

If a man had six camels and wanted to count how many camels he would own if he bought 12 more, he would first put six pebbles in the ones column. Each pebble in that groove would be worth one camel that he already owned.

Then he would put one pebble in the tens groove and two pebbles in the ones column for the 12 camels he wanted to buy. When he added them all together, he saw that he now had one pebble worth ten in the tens column, and eight pebbles worth one each in the ones column. He knew he would have 18 camels when he bought 12 more.

As time went on, people needed to find a way to count when there was no sand or dirt in which to make marks. They used beads instead of pebbles and strung them onto wire. This new abacus could be taken with them on their journeys.

An abacus may seem hard to use at first, but once you learn how, you will be able to figure out answers to all kinds of math problems, and it will get easier and faster. Sometimes, in counting contests, people using an abacus can get an answer faster than those using a calculator can!

I have 6 camels.

If I buy 12 more I will have. . .

Try this:
- Learn how to use an abacus. Practice so you can get better and faster at figuring with an abacus.
- Try to beat your friends at figuring problems when they use a calculator and you use an abacus.
- Set up contests to see who can figure the fastest on an abacus.

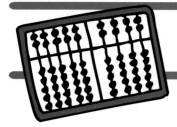

Build an Abacus

Here's an easy way to build your own version of this ancient counting machine.

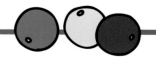

You'll need:

cereal box with the front cut off
10 lengths of thin wire, about 2 inches
    longer than the short end of the box
63 beads that will slide onto the wire
length of ribbon, about 2 inches longer
    than the longest side of the box
hole punch

3. Thread one length of wire through one hole. Place seven beads on the wire inside the box, then pull the end of the wire through the other hole. Wrap the ends of the wire around the holes a few times so it stays in place. Repeat until there is wire in every hole. Leave the sixth wire from the top empty—do not string on beads.

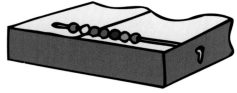

1. With a grown-up's help, punch ten evenly spaced holes on one of the long sides of the box, as shown below.

4. Hold the abacus so there are five beaded wires on top and four beaded wires on the bottom. Push two beads to the right end of each row. Push the other five on each row to the left side.

2. Punch ten evenly spaced holes on the other side, so they are level with the first set of holes.

5. With help, punch a hole in the bottom of the box, about two inches in from the right corner. Punch another hole at the top of the box, about two inches from the right corner.

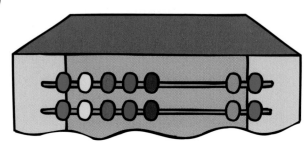

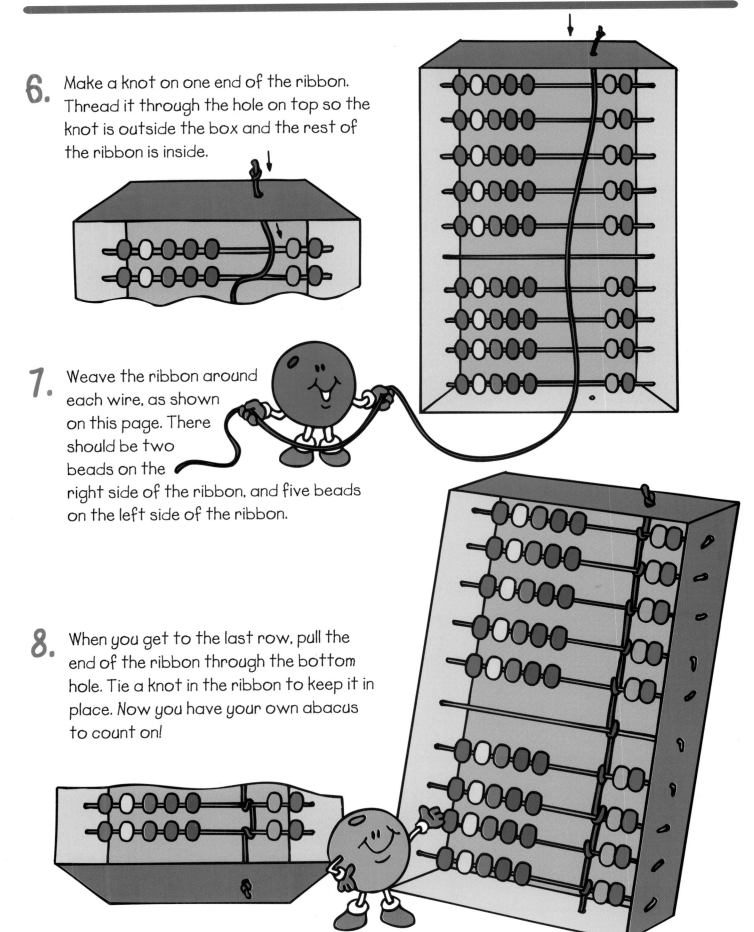

6. Make a knot on one end of the ribbon. Thread it through the hole on top so the knot is outside the box and the rest of the ribbon is inside.

7. Weave the ribbon around each wire, as shown on this page. There should be two beads on the right side of the ribbon, and five beads on the left side of the ribbon.

8. When you get to the last row, pull the end of the ribbon through the bottom hole. Tie a knot in the ribbon to keep it in place. Now you have your own abacus to count on!

Adding It Up—Using An Abacus

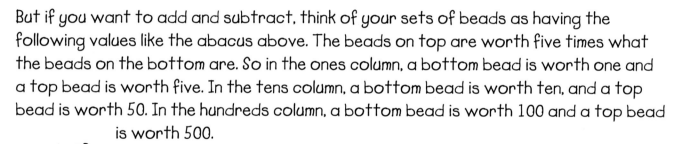

The Heavenly Beads

The Earthly Beads

10,000 1,000 100 10 1 1,000 100 10 1

Adding and subtracting with an abacus can be a little tricky, but keep practicing and you'll get the hang of it.

Hold your abacus so the section with the two beads is at the top and the section with the five beads is at the bottom.

Some people count each set of beads as a place value. Starting at the right side, it would be ones, tens, hundreds, thousands, ten thousands, hundred thousands, etc.

But if you want to add and subtract, think of your sets of beads as having the following values like the abacus above. The beads on top are worth five times what the beads on the bottom are. So in the ones column, a bottom bead is worth one and a top bead is worth five. In the tens column, a bottom bead is worth ten, and a top bead is worth 50. In the hundreds column, a bottom bead is worth 100 and a top bead is worth 500.

To make a number with an abacus you pull the bottom beads up and the top beads down so they meet in the middle.

The bead pulled down in the ones column is worth 5. The bead pulled up in the tens column is worth 10. Together, they make 15.

Try 63 this time:
The three beads pulled up in the ones column are worth 1 each, so they are worth 3 together. The one bead pulled up in the tens column is worth 10. The one bead pulled down in the tens column is worth 50. So 50 + 10 + 3 = 63.

To add on your abacus, you use both sides. To do this, you "transfer" the beads on one side of your abacus to the other. For example, let's say you want to find the answer to 12 + 16. First, set up the number 12 on one side of the empty bar and the number 16 on the other side, as shown.

Now, you "transfer" the beads one column at a time. Start with the ones column on the far right. The beads in the center of that column are worth 6. You need to add 6 to the number 12 on the left side of the abacus. To do this, you push down one bead from the top, and push up one bead from the bottom on the left side of the abacus. Then, clear the ones column on the right side. You added 6 to the left side of the abacus, so you need to take 6 away from the right side.

Finally, transfer the one bead that is pushed up in the tens column on the left to the tens column on the right. Don't forget to clear the tens column on the right when you are finished.

When you count up the beads on the left side, you get 28, and 12 + 16 = 28. You just added with your abacus!

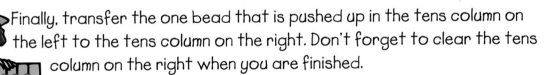

Try this:
- Count to figure out how much all the beads on your abacus are worth.
- Practice adding and subtracting with your abacus.

Bean Collecting

2 players
In this game you won't know who wins until the last second!

You'll need:
paper
pencil
at least 100 dried beans
large piece of poster board (to make
   two gameboards)
4-inch square piece of poster board
paper fastener
scissors

1. Ask a grown-up to help you draw two gameboards like the one shown below on the large piece of poster board. The large squares on the gameboards must be big enough to hold 10 dried beans and the small squares must be big enough to hold one bean.

2. Cut the poster board so you have two separate gameboards.

3. To make a spinner:
- Draw a circle in the middle of the 4-inch square piece of poster board.
- Divide the circle into four equal parts. Then divide each of those parts into three equal parts. Now your spinner has 12 sections.
- Now fill in each section so your spinner looks like the one below.
- Draw an arrow on a piece of poster board like the one below. Cut it out. With help, push the paper fastener through the center of the arrow.
- Poke a hole in the middle of the spinner circle. Push the fastener through the hole and bend the fastener ends so the arrow is attached. Be sure the arrow is loose enough to move freely when you spin it.

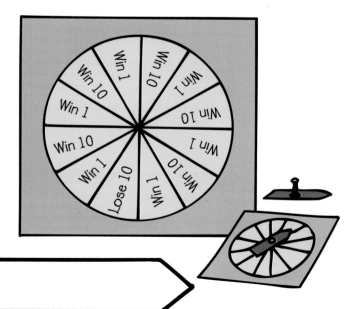

4. Set the gameboard, the bowl of beans, and the spinner on a tabletop.

5. Take turns spinning the spinner. Then follow the directions below:

- When you land on "Win 10" you get ten beans to put in one of your big boxes.

- When you land on "Win 1" you get one bean to put in a little box.

- When you collect ten separate beans in the little boxes, you can move them all to a big box.

- When you land on "Lose 10" you must take ten beans from one of your big boxes and put them back in the bowl. If you don't have ten beans in a big box, you do nothing. (If you have nine separate beans in little boxes, you may keep those.)

6. The winner is the first person to collect 50 beans on his or her board.

Bean Toss

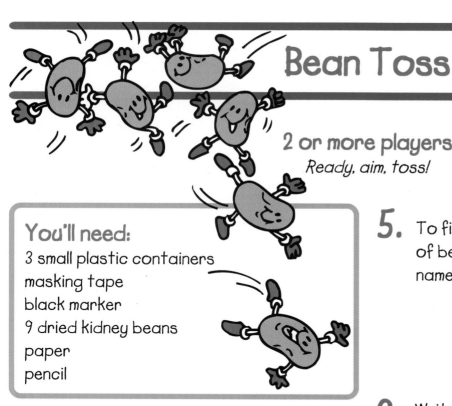

2 or more players

Ready, aim, toss!

You'll need:

3 small plastic containers
masking tape
black marker
9 dried kidney beans
paper
pencil

1. Place a piece of masking tape across the front of each container. On one container, write "Ones." On another container, write "Tens." And on the third container, write "Hundreds."

2. Place the three containers in a row on the floor. Put the Ones container in the front, the Tens container behind it, and the Hundreds container in the back.

3. A few feet away, place a piece of tape on the floor. Now you're ready to play!

4. Without crossing the line, toss nine beans, one at a time, into the containers. If you miss, pick up the bean and throw it again until all the beans are in a container.

5. To figure your score, count the number of beans in each container. Write your name, with three blanks after it, like this:

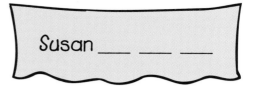

Susan ___ ___ ___

6. Write the number of beans in the Ones container on the right blank. Write the number of beans in the Tens container on the middle blank. Write the number of beans in the Hundreds container on the left blank. This is your score. For example, if you threw four beans into the Ones container, two beans into the Tens container, and three beans into the Hundreds container, your score is 324.

Susan _2_ _1_ _3_

7. Each player takes a turn throwing the beans. The winner is the player with the highest score.

ArithmeTRICK: Paper Folds

You'll need:
a piece of paper

1. Fold the paper in half. Fold it in half again. Fold it in half again seven more times. Does it get easier or harder to fold the paper each time?

   When you fold paper the first time, you make two sheets. When you fold it the second time, you make four. The third time, you make eight sheets. By the time you get to the seventh fold, you have 128 sheets! After the ninth fold, it's like trying to fold a novel in half.

   Try this trick with different sizes and thicknesses of paper. Challenge your friends and family to try folding the paper more than nine times.

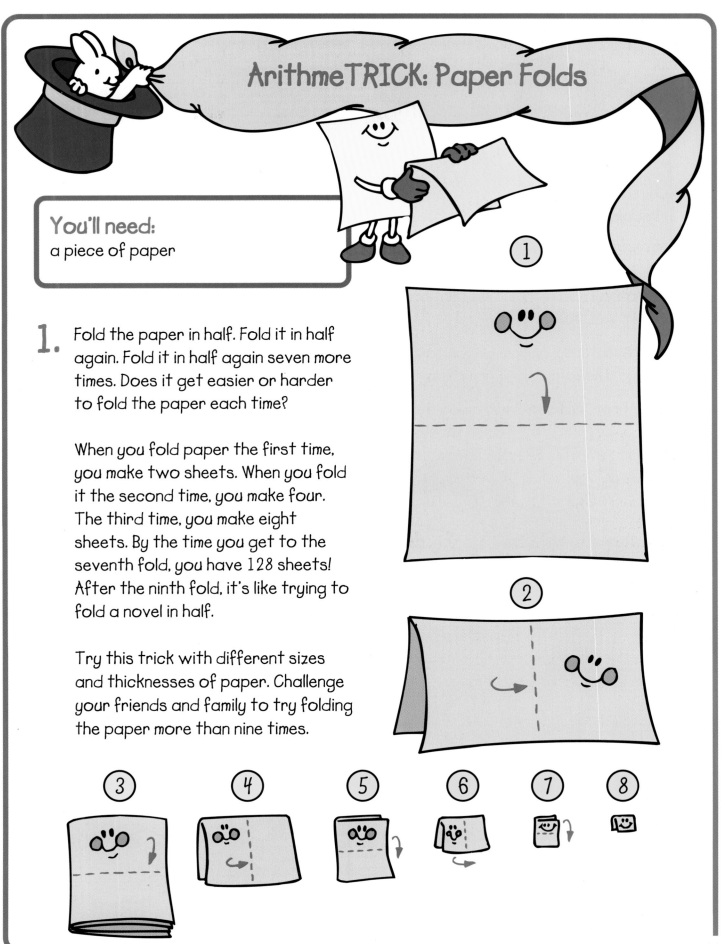

Adding It Up—Who Counted First?

People didn't always use numbers. A long time ago, they didn't even count!

In prehistoric times, people didn't need to count. They didn't keep track of the time of day or what month it was. These things didn't exist. They owned very little, and spent their time hunting for food, making clothing, and building shelter. That was it.

But eventually, people began taking care of herds of animals. They needed some way to keep track of how many animals they had.

The first "numbers" were fingers. When people needed to count their sheep, they would touch each sheep with a finger. If they touched their sheep later in that day and used only seven fingers instead of eight, they knew one sheep had wandered off.

Sometimes they wouldn't have enough fingers for all their animals. So they would use a bag of pebbles or they would scratch one mark into a twig for each sheep.

But they still didn't have any words for counting. If they had five sheep, they might say they had one "hand" (or the word they used for hand) of sheep. Or they might say they had "many" or a "few."

When people first started giving numbers names, they used words that already existed. For example, for the number 2, they might use the word for legs, because humans have two legs. For 4, they might use the word for a fruit that grew in groups of four.

Finally, people put the numbers in order. They gave the first ten numbers special names. The names of the other numbers were based on these first ten. Ten was important because they had ten fingers, and that's how they had always counted. The number "11" means 10 with 1 left over. "Twelve" means 10 with 2 left over. "Twenty" means two 10s. "Thirty" means three 10s. And so on, and so on.

But counting did not stop there. It can take a long time to count things one by one. Almost immediately, people began inventing "counting machines." They started with notches in the stick, went to the abacus, moved on to the calculator, and now use very sophisticated computers.

Try this:
• Make up your own names for the first 20 numbers.

Haikus

A haiku is a poem from Japan that does not rhyme. It has only three lines— the first line has five syllables; the second line has seven syllables, and the third line has five syllables. The poem is usually about nature.

You'll need:

paper
pencil

The sun is setting.
The world gets dark and more still.
Night is here. Day ends.

1. Write the first line of a poem with five syllables. (A syllable is a part of a word. The word cat has only one syllable. The word happy has two syllables. You can tell how many syllables a word has by counting the number of "beats" you hear when you say it.)

2. Write the second line of the poem, using seven syllables.

3. Write the last line of your poem, using five syllables.
Example:
The sun is setting,
The world gets dark and more still.
Night is here. Day ends.

Coin Toss

2 players

Toss a penny and earn "paper clip points" to beat your opponent.

You'll need:
piece of paper
marker
paper clips
2 pennies

4. Play as long as you like, or until all the paper clips are gone. When you are finished, each player counts her paper clips out loud. The player with the most paper clips wins.

1. With help, divide one piece of paper into eight equal sections. Ask a grown-up to randomly pick eight numbers between 1 and 10. Write one number in each box.

2. Both players sit on the floor with the gameboard between them. Sit as close to or as far from the gameboard as you want, but you both must sit the same distance from the board.

3. Take turns throwing your pennies onto the number boxes. Take that number of paper clips from the box. Count out loud as you take the paper clips. If you don't land on the board or land on a line, throw again until you land in one of the boxes.

Counting Book

*Use pictures of your
favorite things to practice counting.*

You'll need:
Polaroid® camera with film
one 8 1/2-inch by 11-inch piece of
    construction paper for every
    two pictures
glue
marker
hole puncher
yarn
scissors

1. With a grown-up's help, use the camera to take a picture of ONE thing—maybe your dog. Then take a picture of two things—like your brother's two turtles. Then take a picture of three things—like your three favorite toy cars. Keep going until you get to the number you want. You can use anything—balls of yarn, spoons, pots and pans, bars of soap, flowers, and more.

2. Ask your grown-up helper to cut the construction-paper sheets in half so they are 8 1/2 inches by 5 1/2 inches.

3. Glue one photo onto each piece of paper. Under each photo, write the number of things that are in the picture.

4. Stack the pages in order. Ask your helper to punch two holes on the left side of your book. Run the yarn through the holes and tie it in a bow to hold your book together. Decorate cover.

A Matched Set

2 players
Can you copy a grown-up's mat creation?

You'll need:
2 file folders
set of small items, like dried beans, buttons, milk jug caps—each player needs the same amount

1. Open the file folder on the floor.

2. Ask a grown-up to arrange her small pieces any way she wants on her side of the folder.

3. When your helper is done, count out loud the number of things on her side of the mat.

4. On your side of the mat, copy your helper's design with your items. When you are finished, count your pieces out loud to see if you used the same number in your design.

Math Giggles
Q: What did one math book say to the other?
A: "I've got problems."

Adding It Up—
Fun, Fabulous, Fascinating Fibonacci

Leonardo Fibonacci was born in Pisa, Italy, around 1175. When he was a boy, his father was a customs official and the family lived in Algeria. That's in Africa.

In Italy, people still counted using Roman numerals. But in Algeria, they used Hindu-Arabic numbers (1, 2, 3, 4, 5, etc.). Leonardo liked these new numbers. He wanted to share them with the people of Italy. In 1202, he wrote a book called *Liber Abaci*, which means, "Book of the Abacus."

In the book, he explained these new numbers and showed the readers how to use them to figure out everyday math problems.

Fibonacci Numbers

1, 1, 2, 3, 5, 8, 13, 21, 34, 55, 89...

Leonardo (who is sometimes called Leonardo of Pisa) also "discovered" a sequence of numbers. The sequence begins like this: 1, 1, 2, 3, 5, 8, 13, 21…. Can you figure out what the next number is?

To find the next Fibonacci number, you add the last two numbers in the sequence together. So after 21 comes 34 (13 + 21 = 34) and after 34 comes 55. It goes on to infinity. The numbers in this sequence are also called Fascinating Fibonaccis.

The thing that is most interesting is that Fibonacci numbers can be found a lot in nature. The pine needles on a pine tree often come in clusters of 2, 3, or 5. The number of spirals on a pinecone is usually one of the Fibonacci numbers. So are the leaves on palm trees, artichokes, pineapples, and sunflowers. If you cut open a fruit or vegetable that has seeds in the middle, the number of sections will also probably be one of these numbers.

Try this:
- See how much of the Fibonacci number sequence you can figure out. Use a calculator if you need to.
- Ask a grown-up to help you cut open some fruits and vegetables that have seeds in the middle, like tomatoes, cucumbers, pears, and apples. How many seeds or sections of seeds do you see? Is this a Fibonacci number?

The Last Cent

2 to 3 players

Pennies aren't just pocket change—they can also be part of a fun and challenging game.

You'll need:
25 pennies

1. Place the pennies in a pile in the middle of a table.

2. Take turns removing pennies from the pile. You must take either one, two, or three pennies each time. You can take a different amount each time or the same amount—you decide.

3. The player who takes the last penny wins.

To change the game, just change the number of pennies in the pile. Or change the number of pennies you may take during each turn—make it only three or four. Or make the person who takes the last penny the loser.

Math Giggles

Q: What happened when the teacher put a plant in the math classroom?

A: It grew square roots.

Marble Trays

2 players

Who will be the first player to use all her marbles?

You'll need:
pair of dice
2 ice cube trays with ¹/₂-inch round holes
bowl
enough marbles to fill both trays

1. Each player gets one of the ice cube trays.

2. Take turns rolling the dice. Whatever number you roll, place that many marbles in your ice cube tray, placing one marble in each section. Be sure to count your marbles out loud as you put them into the tray.

3. The first player to fill her tray is the winner.

2 or 4 players
Will you have the luck of the draw?

You'll need:
a deck of playing cards

For this game,
 a king counts as 13,
 a queen counts as 12,
 and a jack counts as 11.

1. Shuffle the cards. Place them facedown in the middle of the table so all the players can reach them.

2. While turning over the first 13 cards, count from 1 to 13. If you turn over a card that has the same number as the one you are saying at that moment, you get to keep the card. For example, if you say "2," and the card in your hand is the 5 of diamonds, you don't keep that card. If you say "6," and the card in your hand is the 6 of hearts, you keep that card.

3. Take turns drawing 13 cards until all the cards have been turned over.

4. At the end of the game, each player adds up the value of his cards. So if you have a king, a 2, and a 6, you add 13 + 2 + 6 = 21. The player with the most points wins.

. . . 5, 6!

Adding & Subtracting

You can learn to add and subtract with a little practice. And practice can be fun! Try one of the exciting games of luck, chance, and skill in this section. You'll have such a good time, you won't believe you're solving math problems! Soon you'll be adding and subtracting like a pro. Fun and games and math–it all adds up!

Bean Bingo

2 or more players
To get Bingo, you must solve some problems first!

You'll need:
package of dried beans
at least 24 index cards
black marker
four 8½-inch by 11-inch
   pieces of cardboard

2. On each index card, write a different math problem using the numbers 0 to 10. The answers to the problems must be 0 to 10.

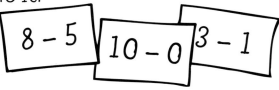

8 – 5   10 – 0   3 – 1

1. Use the marker to divide each piece of cardboard into 30 equal squares, as shown below. In the first row of boxes on each cardboard piece, write B-I-N-G-O. In the rest of the boxes, write the numbers 1 through 10, in random order.

3. Each player gets a bingo card. The index cards are placed in a stack facedown.

4. Players take turns drawing the top index card in the deck. Help each other solve the problem. Place a bean on the answer if you have it on your bingo card.

5. The first player to get five in a row, column, or diagonal calls out, "Bingo!" and wins the game.

B	I	N	G	O
10	2	3	7	8
1	6	5	3	6
2	7	1	2	7
8	4	3	4	1
5	9	10	9	4

Tug-of-War

2 players

For this tug-of-war, a strong brain is more important than strong arms.

You'll need:
18-inch length of yarn
washer
8½-inch by 12-inch piece of
    cardboard
black marker
1 die

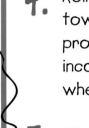

4. Roll the die and move the washer toward your finish line. Answer the problem that you land on. If you are incorrect, move the washer back to where you started.

5. The winner is the first person to get the washer to his finish line.

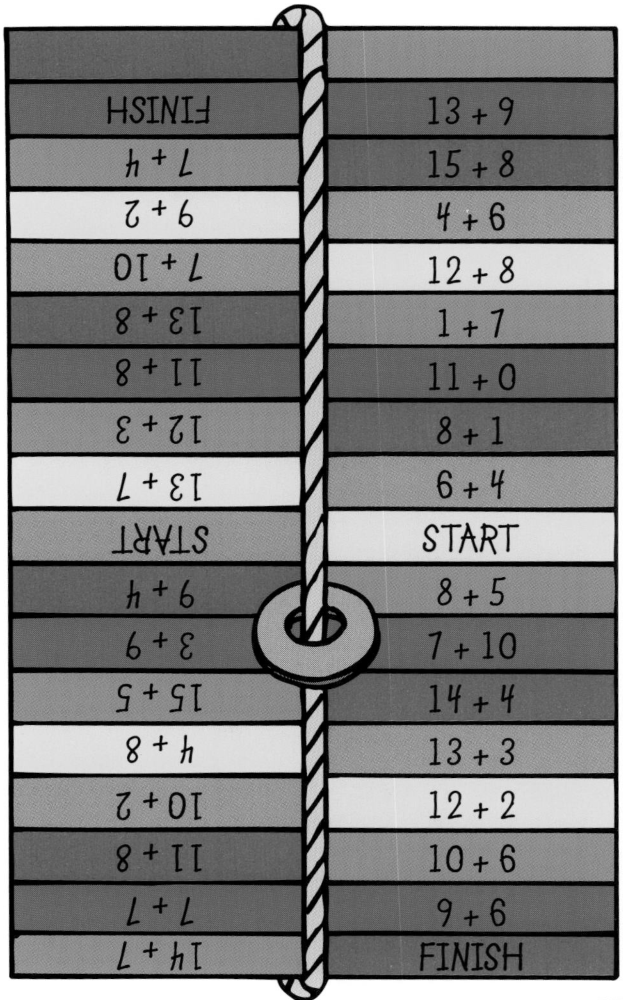

1. Ask a grown-up to help you use the cardboard and marker to make a gameboard that looks like the one on the right. If those problems are too easy or too hard, use your math book to find other ones. With help, make an answer key for the problems you choose.

2. Thread the yarn through the washer. Tie the yarn around the gameboard, as shown on the right. Make the yarn loose enough so that you can move the washer, but tight enough to stay on the board.

3. To play the game, each player chooses a side of the gameboard. (Your side is the one where the math problems are NOT upside down when you look at them). Players sit with the board between them.

(left side)	(right side)
FINISH	13 + 9
7 + 4	15 + 8
9 + 2	4 + 6
7 + 10	12 + 8
13 + 8	1 + 7
11 + 8	11 + 0
12 + 3	8 + 1
13 + 7	6 + 4
START	START
9 + 4	8 + 5
3 + 9	7 + 10
15 + 5	14 + 4
4 + 8	13 + 3
10 + 2	12 + 2
11 + 8	10 + 6
7 + 7	9 + 6
14 + 7	FINISH

ArithmeTRICK: This is the One

The answer to this puzzle will always be 1.

You'll need:
pencil
paper
calculator

1. Pick any number.

2. Add 3 to that number.

3. Double that number.

4. Subtract 4 from that number.

5. Divide that answer by 2.

6. Subtract the first number you chose.

$$25$$

$$25 + 3 = 28$$

$$28 + 28 = 56$$

$$56 - 4 = 52$$

$$\begin{array}{r} 26 \\ 2\overline{)52} \end{array}$$

$$26 - 25 = 1$$

Sock Hop Math

2 players and 1 caller

Hop to it! Jump on the right answer and you could win the game.

You'll need:
old bedsheet
thick, black permanent marker
at least 20 index cards
dried beans or play coins
2 different-colored paper cups

1. Write the numbers 0 through 9 on a bedsheet as shown below. (You can write each number more than once.) Spread the bedsheet on the floor in an open area.

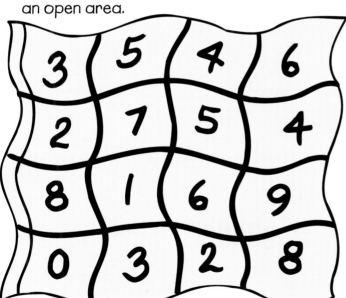

3	5	4	6
2	7	5	4
8	1	6	9
0	3	2	8

2. On the index cards, write math problems with answers from 0 to 9.

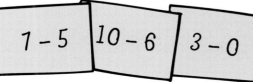

7 – 5   10 – 6   3 – 0

3. One person is the caller. Each player labels a colored cup and puts it on the floor by the caller. The caller shuffles the index cards, draws a card, and reads the math problem.

Patty   Carl

7 – 5 = ?

4. The other two players figure out the answer and then jump onto that number. The caller puts a dried bean in the cup of the player who lands on the correct number first.

5. The player with the most beans in her cup at the end of the game is the winner.

Tic-Fact-Toe

2 players
Try this new twist on tic-tac-toe.

You'll need:
paper
pencil
2 dice
red pen
black pen

1. Draw a regular tic-tac-toe grid. Choose nine numbers from 2 to 12 and put one in each space. (Do not repeat any numbers.)

2. One player uses the black pen and one player uses the red pen. Take turns rolling the dice. When it is *your* turn, add together the two numbers on the dice. If that answer is on the grid, put an "X" through it with your pen. Then the other player rolls the dice and does the same thing.

3. The first player to get three Xs in a row wins the round and gets one point. Play as many rounds as you like. The winner of the game is the player who earns the most points.

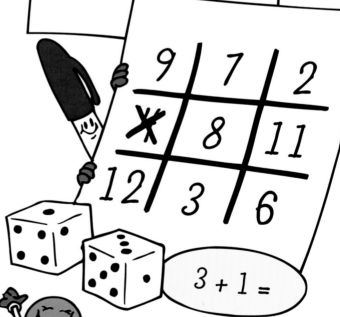

$$2 + 3 =$$

2	9	12
4	6	10
11	8	X

9	7	2
X	8	11
12	3	6

$$3 + 1 =$$

Math Giggles
Q: How many peas are there in a pod?
A: One p.

Sum It Up

2 or more players

*Draw the high pair and you're on your way
to the winner's circle!*

You'll need:
1 deck of playing cards
pencil
paper

1. Remove the kings, queens, jacks, and aces from the deck of cards. Shuffle the cards. Place the deck facedown on the table.

2. Take turns drawing two cards. Turn over your cards and add them together. Say the sum out loud.

3. When everyone has picked two cards and announced a sum, the person with the highest number gets everyone's cards. If two or more people get the same answer, all players keep their own cards.

4. Keep drawing cards until there are none left. The player with the most cards is the winner.

Tip: You can also subtract your lower card from your higher card and give the cards to the player with the smallest answer.

$3 + 2 = 5$

$2 + 2 = 4$

$2 + 5 = 7$

Snakes

2 or more players

Seven slithery snakes send senses scrambling.

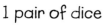

You'll need:

1 pair of dice
1 pencil for each player
1 sheet of paper for each player

1. Everyone should write the numbers 2 through 12, except for 7, on his paper.

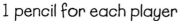

2, 3, 4, 5, 6, 8, 9, 10, 11, 12

2. Taking turns, each player rolls the dice. When you roll the dice, add the two numbers on the dice together. Cross out that number on your paper—the other players do not cross out this number. If that number has already been crossed out, do nothing.

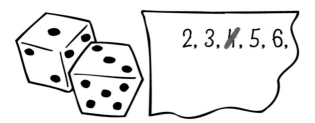

2, 3, 4, 5, 6,

3. If you roll a 7, draw a snake on your paper. If you get seven snakes on your paper, you are out of the game.

2, 3, 4, 5, 6, 8, 9, 10, 11, 12

4. The winner is the first player to cross out all the numbers on his paper, or the only player without seven snakes.

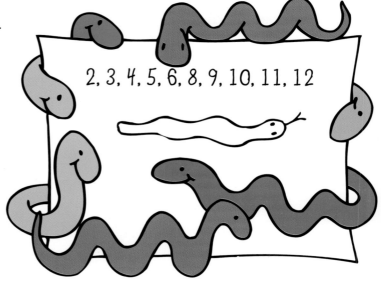

2, 3, 4, 5, 6, 8, 9, 10, 11, 12

ArithmeTRICK: 6174

You'll need:
pencil
paper
calculator to check
    your work

Eventually, you will get 6174 as the answer to this trick.

1. Pick four numbers from 0 to 9:

6, 1, 8, 5

2. Put them in order from largest to smallest.

8651

3. Put them in order from smallest to largest.

1568

4. Subtract the small number from the large number:

$$\begin{array}{r} 8651 \\ -\ 1568 \\ \hline 7083 \end{array}$$

5. Order the numbers in that answer from largest to smallest.

8730

6. Order the numbers in that answer from smallest to largest.

0378

7. Subtract the smaller number from the larger:

$$\begin{array}{r} 8730 \\ -\ 0378 \\ \hline 8352 \end{array}$$

8. Continue Steps 5 through 7 until you get the answer 6174.

$$\begin{array}{r} 8532 \\ -\ 2358 \\ \hline 6174 \end{array}$$

Disappearing Ten

2 or more players

Can you subtract your paper clips faster than everyone else?

You'll need:

one 8 1/2-inch by 11-inch
    sheet of paper for
    each player
pencil
10 paper clips for
    each player
1 die

1. Draw a gameboard like the one below for each player.

2. Put one paper clip in each box on your board.

3. Take turns rolling the die. After you have rolled a number, take that number of paper clips off your board.

4. If you roll a number that is greater than the number of paper clips you have left, you do nothing. That means you must roll a number that is less than or the same as the number of paper clips you have. For example, if you have three paper clips on your board and you roll a 4, you do nothing. If you have three paper clips on your board and you roll a 2, you take two paper clips off your board. Then you must roll a 1, and only a 1, to win.

5. The winner is the first player who subtracts all her paper clips.

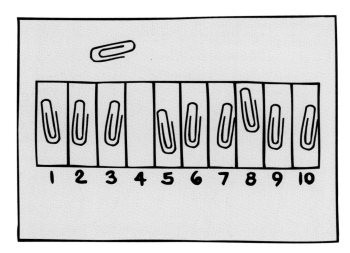

74

Sum Building

2 to 4 players

Do you know what your opponents will do before they do it?

You'll need:
one 8½-inch by 11-inch piece
    of paper
25 dried beans or pennies
piece of scrap paper
pencil

1. With a grown-up's help, make a board like the one below on the piece of paper.

5	5	5	5	5
4	4	4	4	4
3	3	3	3	3
2	2	2	2	2
1	1	1	1	1

2. Choose a number between 25 and 55. This is your goal number.

3. Take turns covering one of the numbers on the board with a penny. Keep track of the total sum of the covered numbers.

For example, if the first player covers a 3, the sum is 3. If the next player covers a 1, then the sum of 3 and 1 is 4. If the third player covers a 2, the sum of 4 and 2 is 6, and so on. Write the sum on scrap paper if you think you will forget it.

4. The winner is the player who reaches the goal number.

Checkered Math

2 players
Here's a whole new way to play checkers.

You'll need:
checkerboard
checkers
paper
scissors
pen
clear tape

1. Ask a grown-up to tape small pieces of white paper over the black squares of a checkerboard. Tell your helper to write a math problem on each paper. If you want, you can make up an answer key.

2. You play Checkered Math just like regular checkers. However, when you move a checker to a new square, you must solve the problem. If you solve the problem incorrectly, you move your checker back to where it came from and lose your turn.

3. The winner is the player who is left with the most checkers.

4 + 4

6

1 + 3

7 − 2

Math Giggles
Q: When do 2 and 2 make more than 4?
A: When they are 22.

Six Dominoes

2 to 4 players

Use your dominoes to earn the most points in this game of skill.

You'll need:

dominoes
paper
pencil

1. Place all the dominoes facedown on the table. Each player chooses six dominoes. Don't show them to the other players! Choose one person to keep track of the score.

2. The first player puts one domino faceup in the center of the table.

3. The next player must place a domino next to the first domino, so that the two ends that are touching have a sum of 6. (See the examples below.)

4. To score—Draw a score sheet like the one below. Each time a player adds a domino to the table, her score is the number of dots that are on the domino. If a player uses all her dominoes, she gets 10 bonus points.

Janie	Billy	Tiffany
9	7	6
+ 5	+ 8	+ 7
14	15	13

5. Players take turns adding dominoes. If you don't have a domino you can use, take one from the facedown pile on the table. Keep taking dominoes until you find one you can use. If you draw every facedown domino and can't find one to use, you pass.

6. The game is over when one player has used all her dominoes, or no players can make a move. The winner is the player with the most points.

> **Tip:** Instead of adding the dominoes together to get 6, try subtracting one from the other to get 1.

ArithmeTRICK: Nothing Left

The answer to this puzzle will always be 0.

You'll need:
pencil
paper

1. Pick ANY four-digit number.

2. Find the difference between each neighboring number.

3. Find the difference between the first and last digits in the number.

4. In this example, the new number is 1373. Continue Steps 2 and 3 until you have all zeros.

1. 6529

2. 6 − 5 = 1
   5 − 2 = 3
   9 − 2 = 7

3. 9 − 6 = 3

4. 1373

1373→2442→2020→2222→0000

Tic-Card-Toe

2 players
This tic-tac-toe is a game of luck and chance.

You'll need:
1 deck of cards
pencil
paper

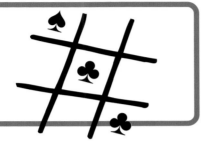

1. Shuffle the cards. Place nine cards facedown in three rows.

2. Take turns turning over the cards. You want to get three cards of the same color in a row, a column, or a diagonal. The first player to do this wins the round.

3. To score, add the numbers of the three winning cards together. If the three cards are all spades, all hearts, all diamonds, or all clubs, double that number for a bonus score. Write the score under the player's name on a piece of paper.

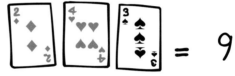 = 9

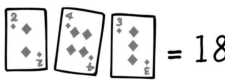 = 18

4. Play more rounds until one player reaches 300. He is the winner.

18!

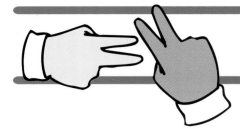

Finger Shoots

2 players

Who has the highest-scoring hands in the land?

You'll need:
your hands
pencil
paper

1. The first player says, "1, 2, 3, shoot!" Both of you hold out any number of fingers that you choose.

2. The first player gets that score. First he adds the number of fingers together. Then he subtracts one number from the other. Then he adds the two numbers together and gets his score.

For example, if you hold out three fingers and the other player holds out five,

he adds:
3 + 5 = 8
Then he subtracts:
5 − 3 = 2
He adds those
two answers together:
8 + 2 = 10
His score is 10.

$$\begin{array}{r} 3 \\ + 5 \\ \hline 8 \end{array} \quad \begin{array}{r} 5 \\ - 3 \\ \hline 2 \end{array} \quad \begin{array}{r} 8 \\ + 2 \\ \hline 10 \end{array}$$

3. Then it is your turn. (You are the second player.) You yell, "1, 2, 3, shoot!" and you both hold out fingers again. This time the score goes to you.

4. If you hold out the same number of fingers as the other player, you add and subtract the same way, but then add on a bonus score of 10.

For example, if you both hold out four fingers:

4 + 4 = 8
4 − 4 = 0
8 + 0 = 8
8 + 10 = 18

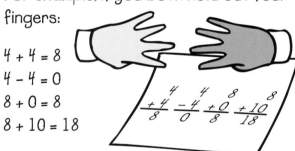

$$\begin{array}{r} 4 \\ + 4 \\ \hline 8 \end{array} \quad \begin{array}{r} 4 \\ - 4 \\ \hline 0 \end{array} \quad \begin{array}{r} 8 \\ + 0 \\ \hline 8 \end{array} \quad \begin{array}{r} 8 \\ + 10 \\ \hline 18 \end{array}$$

5. If you need to, keep track of your points on the paper. The winner is the first player to reach 50 points.

One, two, three, shoot!

Calendar Toss

2 or more players
Some days are just better than others in this basic skills game.

You'll need:
old calendar
nickels or bottle caps
pencil
paper

4. Play as long as you like. The winner is the player with the most points.

1. Tear out a 31-day-month page from the calendar. Lay it on the floor.

2. Stand a few feet away from the calendar page. Take turns tossing your coins or bottle caps onto the calendar.

3. Keep track of your scores with the pencil and paper. You win the same number of points as the number that you land on. If you land on a line between two, three, or four different boxes, add all those numbers together to find your score.

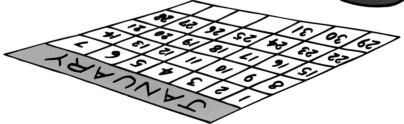

Hit 15

2 players
Are the cards on your side?

You'll need:
1 deck of cards

For this game, the picture cards will count as 5.

1. Place the deck of cards facedown in the middle of the table.

2. One at a time, each player draws three cards. If they equal 15 when added together, she keeps the three cards. If they do not equal 15, she puts them in a discard pile.

3. Take turns until there are no cards left in the deck. Each player counts the number of cards she kept. Score one point for each card. Then play another round.

4. The first player to get 25 points wins the game.

Math Giggles
Q: What odd number becomes even when beheaded?
A: Seven becomes even.

Multiplying & Dividing

Multiplying and dividing get easier the more you practice. They can also save you time. It's so much easier to say 4 x 2 = 8 than 2 + 2 + 2 + 2 = 8. Once you start multiplying, you'll never want to go back to the slow way of figuring things out again.

Adding It Up—Why We Multiply

People haven't been *multiplying* forever. It was something that was invented. There was a time when people could only count, add, and subtract.

This wasn't too bad when they were dealing with small numbers, but it could take hours if they were dealing with bigger numbers!

For example, builders often needed to order materials when they were building stores and houses. They had to figure out how many bricks they needed. But this was hard to do, and they usually just guessed. Whether they guessed too many bricks or too few, it would end up costing time and money.

But then someone had a new idea. In ancient times, people measured sizes by hands and paces. So if a builder knew he was building a wall that was 20 paces high and 30 paces wide, he would draw a grid on a piece of paper. If each brick was one pace long, he would draw a rectangle that was 20 squares high and 30 squares wide. When he counted up all the squares, he knew he needed 600 bricks.

Those builders thought they were just counting. But they were multiplying in a way. Multiplying is just a fast way of counting. For example, when you say "5 x 9," you are saying, "What do five 9s add up to [9 + 9 + 9 + 9 + 9]?"

In the 1400s, someone finally sat down and drew a square that had ten squares across and ten squares down. That person filled in the squares with numbers. This was the first multiplication table.

People who worked with numbers a lot carried a copy of the multiplication table around with them, so they could look up the answers they needed. It was like the calculators or computers that we use today.

We don't carry around the multiplication table anymore. We memorize it when we are in school. We keep it in our heads. Ancient people would be surprised at how quickly you can think of the answer to 8 x 6 or 4 x 9.

Try this:
- Count how many paces long and wide your bedroom is. If you needed to order bricks that were one pace long, how many would you need?
- Try figuring out multiplication problems the old-fashioned way. Draw a grid and count the boxes.

The Multiplication Table

To use the multiplication table:
- Decide what two numbers you want to multiply.
- Find the first number in the left-hand column.
- Find the second number in the top row.
- Drag your finger across the row from the first number until you reach the column where the second number is found. The number where that column and row meet is the answer.

1 x 1 =

	0	1	2
0	0	0	0
1	0	1	2
2	0	2	4

	0	1	2	3	4	5	6	7	8	9	10
0	0	0	0	0	0	0	0	0	0	0	0
1	0	1	2	3	4	5	6	7	8	9	10
2	0	2	4	6	8	10	12	14	16	18	20
3	0	3	6	9	12	15	18	21	24	27	30
4	0	4	8	12	16	20	24	28	32	36	40
5	0	5	10	15	20	25	30	35	40	45	50
6	0	6	12	18	24	30	36	42	48	54	60
7	0	7	14	21	28	35	42	49	56	63	70
8	0	8	16	24	32	40	48	56	64	72	80
9	0	9	18	27	36	45	54	63	72	81	90
10	0	10	20	30	40	50	60	70	80	90	100

Seeing Stars

2 players

A couple of lucky throws makes you the winner.

You'll need:
paper for each player
pencil for each player
dice

5. Play again until one of you wins five rounds.

1. Taking turns, each player rolls the dice twice.

2. After the first roll, draw that many circles on your paper.

3. After the second roll, draw that many stars inside each circle.

4. Count your stars. The player with the most stars wins the round.

Math Giggles

Q: How many times can you subtract 10 from 100?

A: Just once. After that you are subtracting 10 from a number other than 100.

87

Boxes, Boxes Everywhere

2 players
Can you build the biggest box?

You'll need:
graph paper with ¹/₄-inch squares
2 pencils
1 die

1. Each player gets a piece of graph paper and a pencil. Take turns throwing the die. The object of the game is to draw the biggest box.

2. Your first throw decides how long your box will be. For example, if you throw a 5, draw a line that is five boxes long on your graph paper.

3. The second throw decides how high your box will be. For example, if you throw a 3, draw a line that is three boxes high, connecting it to one end of your first line (see below). Draw the lines that will complete the box (see the dotted lines below).

4. The winner is the player with the biggest box. To double-check the size of the boxes, count the number of squares inside. Then, multiply the first number you rolled by the second number you rolled. What do you notice about these numbers?

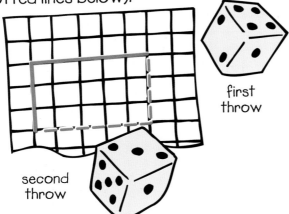

first throw

second throw

ArithmeTRICK: Magic Fingers

Try multiplying by nine on your fingers.

You'll need:
Your hands

1. Place your hands on the table in front of you. Spread out your fingers.

2. Number your fingers in order from 1 to 10.

3. Pick a number from 1 to 10. Let's say you pick 6.

4. Using your fingers, multiply 6 x 9. Fold down finger 6.

5. Count the fingers remaining to the left of finger number 6.

6. Count the number of fingers on the right side of finger 6.

7. Write down the number of fingers on your left hand. Next to it write the number of fingers on the right. You will have the answer to the multiplication problem. 9 x 6 = 54

Adding It Up–Baseball Stats

If you don't like math very much, remember that it is a big part of some very important daily tasks. Like figuring out baseball stats!

Batting Averages

Your batting average tells people how often you hit the ball when you're at bat. For major league players, a really good hitter will have around a .300 average. A GREAT hitter will be close to .400. Believe it or not, Little League baseball players can have higher averages than professional players. Some Little Leaguers have .700 or .800 averages!

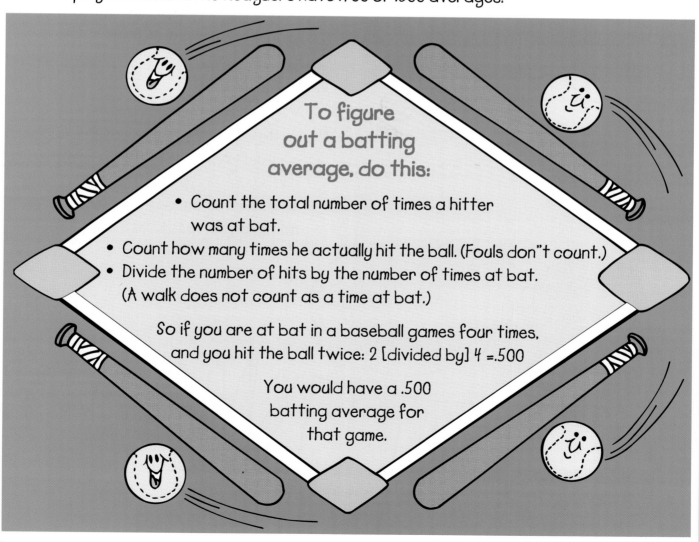

To figure out a batting average, do this:

- Count the total number of times a hitter was at bat.
- Count how many times he actually hit the ball. (Fouls don"t count.)
- Divide the number of hits by the number of times at bat. (A walk does not count as a time at bat.)

So if you are at bat in a baseball games four times, and you hit the ball twice: 2 [divided by] 4 =.500

You would have a .500 batting average for that game.

Baseball batting averages are written with decimals. A decimal looks like a period and you will see it in the middle of a bunch of numbers, like this:

345.67

You would say "three hundred forty-five point six seven." The "six seven" stands for a fraction. It's not a whole one. It's 67/100 of one.

But you don't pronounce the decimal in batting averages. If someone had a .200 batting average, you'd say she had a "two hundred average."

BATTING AVERAGE

Times at bat:
4
Times hit the ball:
2

$$4\overline{)2}$$ = .500

Try this:
• Go outside with a Wiffle® bat and ball. Ask a grown-up to pitch to you five times. Figure out your batting average.

Triplet Books

Make a little booklet that holds dozens of practice math problems.

You'll need:

one 8$\frac{1}{2}$-inch by 11-inch sheet of construction paper
two 8$\frac{1}{2}$-inch by 11-inch sheets of white paper
stapler or yarn
pencil
ruler
scissors
marker
calculator

1. Place the construction paper down on a table. Lay the white paper on top. Fold all three sheets in half to make a booklet.

2. Ask a grown-up to staple the book at the fold. (Or, tie yarn around the fold to keep the white paper in place.)

3. Using the pencil and the ruler, divide the first booklet page into three equal sections.

4. **STOP** Cut on the lines through all four sheets of paper, to make 12 mini-pages.

5. On the top sections, write one number from 500 to 999 on each page. In the middle sections, write one of these symbols on each page: + − x ÷. On the bottom sections, write one number from 1–499.

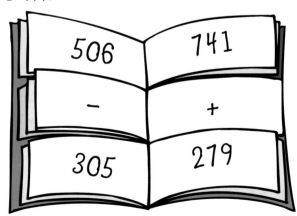

6. Practice your math by flipping the pages of the booklet to create different problems. Figure out the answers, and then check your work with a calculator.

ArithmeTRICK: Your Birth Day

Figure out what day of the week you were born.

You'll need:
pencil
paper
calculator

1. Let's say your birthday is September 30, 1970. Let A be the year in which you were born.
A=1970

2. Let B be the day of the year that you were born.
January, March, May, July, August, October, December = 31 days
February = 28 days (29 days in a leap year)
April, June, September, November = 30 days
So for September 30, the answer found like this:
31 + 28 + 31 + 30 + 31 + 30 + 31 + 31 + 30 = 273rd day of the year
B=273

3. Find C: C=(A−1) ÷ 4. Leave off the remainder.
C= (1970 −1) ÷ 4
C =1969 ÷ 4
C = 492

4. Find D: D = A + B + C
D=1970 + 273 + 492
D = 2735

5. For this step, do not use a calculator. Divide D by 7. Notice the remainder. (Do not use decimal number.) 2735 ÷ 7 = 390 r. 5

6. Match the remainder to one of the days of the week below. That is the day you were born:
0 Friday
1 Saturday
2 Sunday
3 Monday
4 Tuesday
5 Wednesday
6 Thursday

So a person born on September 30, 1970, was born on a Wednesday.

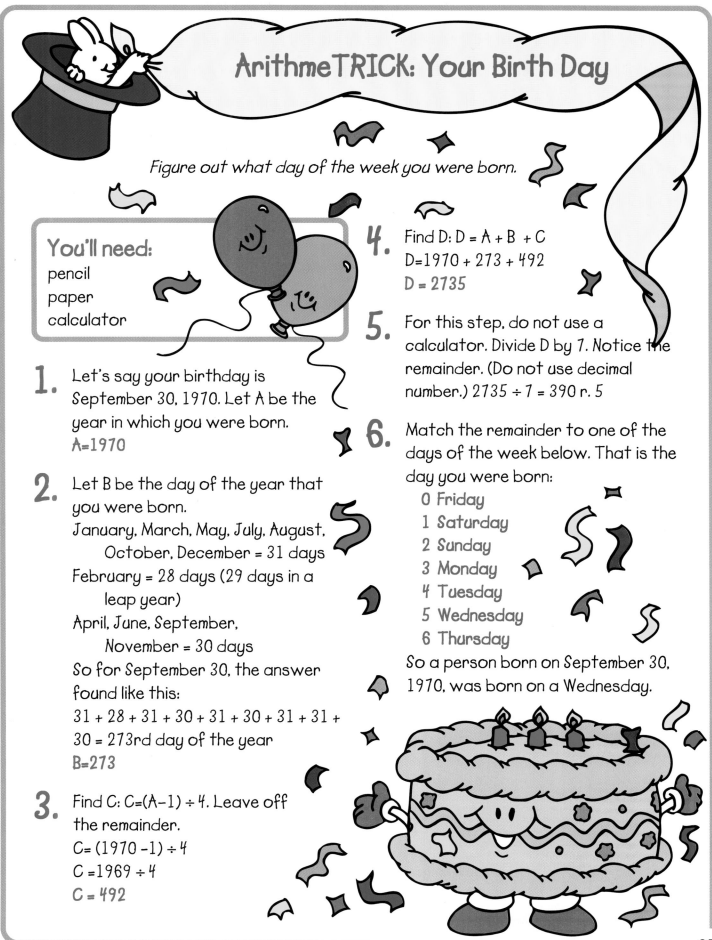

Size, Shape, & Space

Everything you see has some kind of shape. And has some kind of size. And takes up space. You may not understand what this has to do with numbers. But once you understand the ideas of size, shape, and space, it will be easier to imagine certain math concepts.

Make a Puzzle

Make your own puzzle and see if you can put it back together!

You'll need:
cardboard (any size)
paint
paintbrush
scissors

1. Paint one side of the cardboard with one color. Let it dry.

2. STOP Cut the cardboard into pieces. Do this by making big cuts across one section at a time, as shown below.

3. Now put the puzzle back together. The more cuts you make, the more difficult the puzzle will be.

Adding It Up—Shapes to Know

SQUARE
a playing die

CONE
an ice-cream cone
a clown's hat

DIAMOND
a baseball field

OCTAGON
a stop sign

STOP

CUBE
a toy block

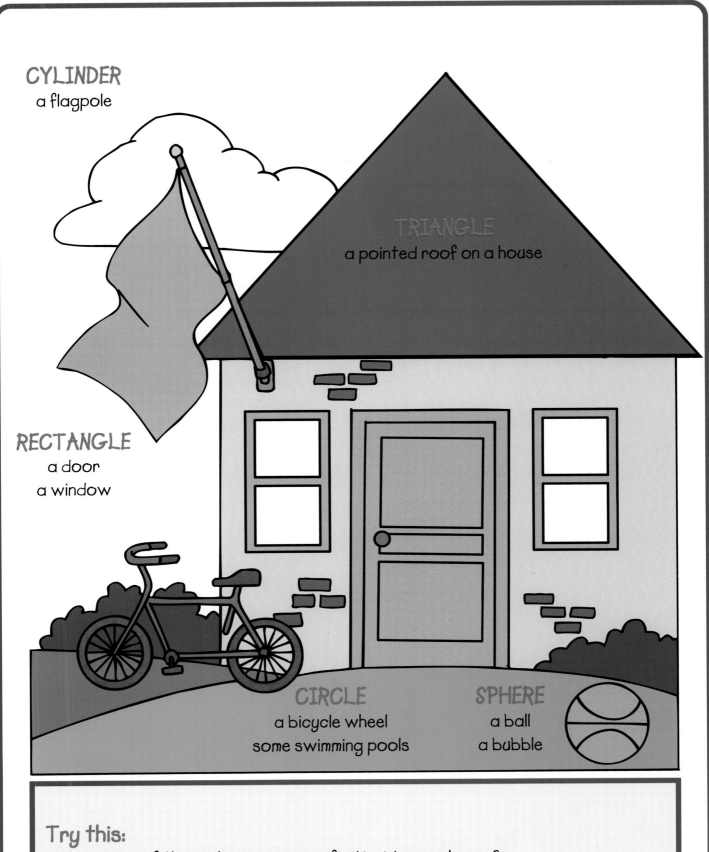

CYLINDER
a flagpole

TRIANGLE
a pointed roof on a house

RECTANGLE
a door
a window

CIRCLE
a bicycle wheel
some swimming pools

SPHERE
a ball
a bubble

Try this:
• How many of these shapes can you find inside your house?

Tangrams

These puzzles are traditional math games.

You'll need:
poster board
scissors
pencils

1. Ask a grown-up to make a photocopy of the shapes below.

2. **STOP** Cut out the shapes. Lay them on the poster board. Trace around the shapes. Cut out the shapes from the poster board.

3. What kinds of shapes can you make from your tangrams? Try making some of the shapes on the next page. See page 151 for the answers.

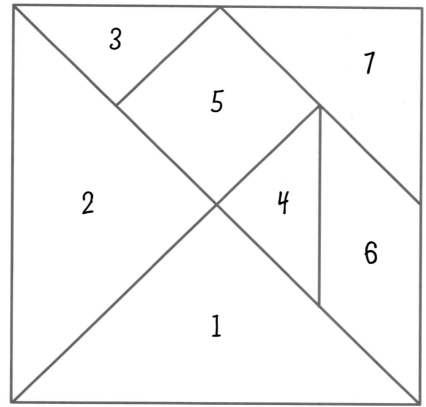

Tangrams come from China. No one is really sure how old they are, but the first time they were mentioned in a book was around 1813. A tangram is made up of seven separate pieces that are called tans. When you put them together to make new shapes and designs, that is a tangram. Napoleon Bonaparte and President John Quincy Adams were among the many fans of tangrams.

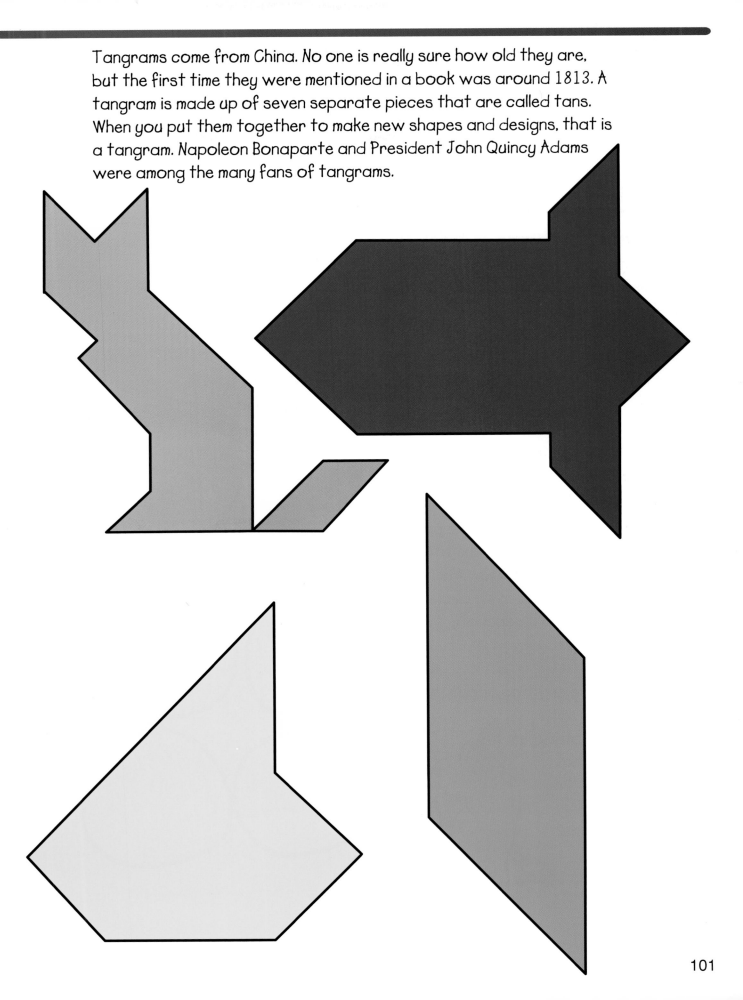

Pasta Pictures

How many different ways can you arrange your ziti?

You'll need:
box of dried ziti
    or another long,
    tube-shaped pasta
construction paper
glue
pencil

1. Pick a number from 3 to 10.

2. Using that number of zitis, see how many shapes you can make from the pasta. Plan your design and glue the ziti to the construction paper. When you finish a design, draw a circle around it to keep it separate from the others.

3. Do you notice anything about the pictures? Do some look bigger or smaller than the others, even though they use the same amount of zitis?

ArithmeTRICK: Connect the Dots

You'll need:

pencils

paper

1. Draw 9 dots in a square.

2. Use four straight lines to connect the dots. Do not lift your pencil from the paper. You may cross over a line, but you cannot retrace a line.

3. Can you find some way to do this besides the solution shown below?

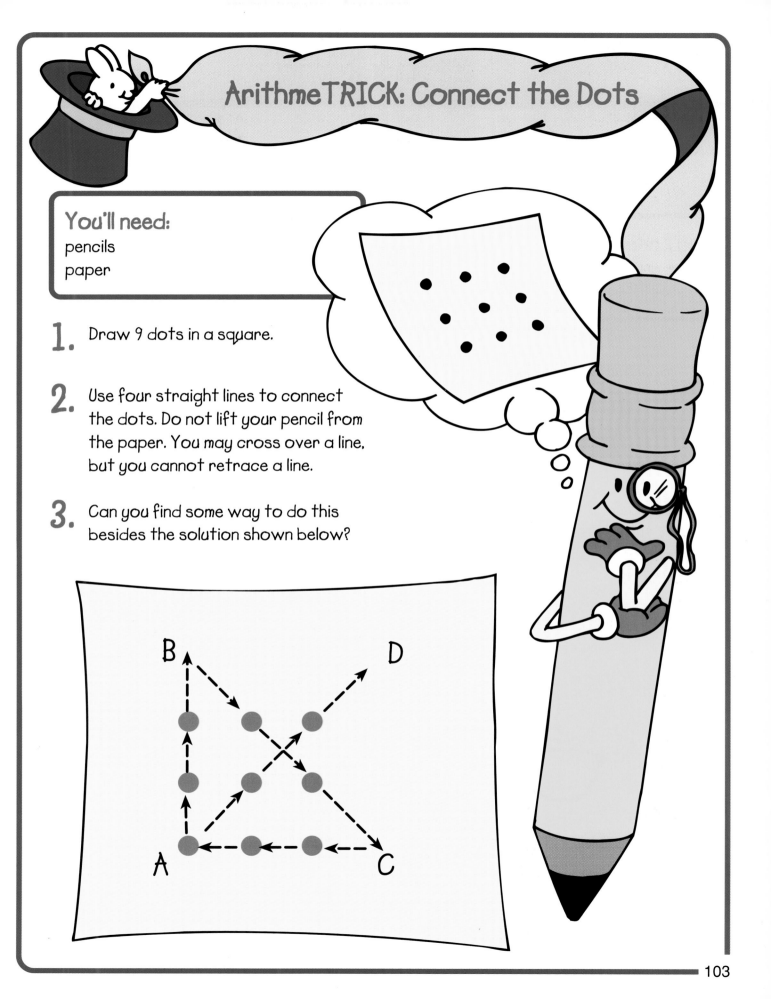

String Thing

2 players

Can you tell how long something is just by looking at it?

You'll need:
string
scissors

1. Walk around your house. Find different objects you'd like to measure.

2. When you find something, study it for a while. Just look–don't touch!

3. When you both are finished studying the item, turn away. Try to cut a piece of string that is the same length or height as the object.

4. The player whose string is closest to the length of the object without being longer wins.

Math Giggles

Q: Use "geometry" in a sentence.

A: When the little acorn grew up, it said, "Geometry!" ("Gee! I'm a tree!")

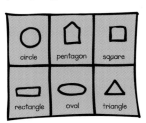

Lotto

2 players

Collect a set of shapes and you win the game.

You'll need:
2 pieces 11-inch by
    14-inch poster board
index cards
scissors
crayons or markers

1. Ask a grown-up to help you make two playing boards like the ones below.

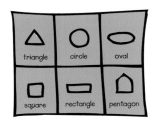

2. 🛑 With help, cut the index cards in half.

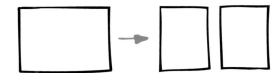

3. On two index cards, write LOSE A TURN. Then make two circle cards, two oval cards, two square cards, two rectangle cards, two triangle cards, and two pentagon cards.

4. Shuffle the cards. Spread them out facedown on the table. Take turns picking a card. Match the card to the same shape on your board. Place the card on top of that shape.

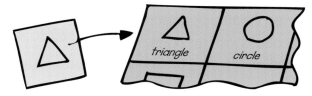

5. If you pick a shape that you already covered, put the card back on the table and mix all the cards up a bit before drawing again. If you choose the LOSE A TURN card, you do not get to cover a shape on that turn. Place the LOSE A TURN card back on the table and mix up the cards.

6. The winner is the first player to cover all six shapes on her lotto board.

NIM Board

2 players
You won't be bored with this board game.

You'll need:
one 8 1/2 inch by 12-inch
    sheet of white paper
black marker
ruler
dried beans, peanuts in the
    shells, or buttons

1. Use the marker and ruler to draw a grid like the one below.

2. Take turns putting beans on the squares. You must put one or two peanuts on the board when it is your turn. There must be one nut per square and they must be next to each other or one on top of the other (not diagonal).

3. The player who fills the last square is the winner.

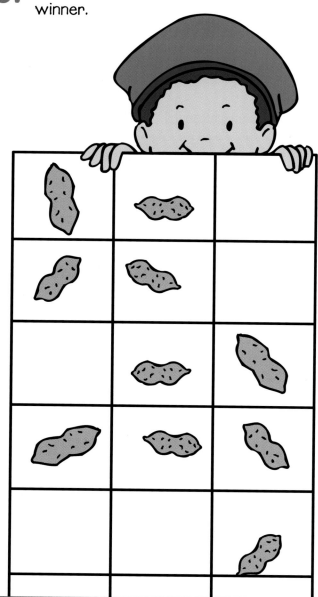

Try making a grid with more or fewer squares for your next game. Or make a rule that you can put one, two, or three beans on the grid during your turn.

Serpent

2 players

Wind your way around and corner your opponent.

You'll need:
paper
pencil

1. Draw 42 dots on your paper as shown.

2. Take turns drawing a line from one dot to another. (Do not draw any diagonal lines.) Your line must be connected to either end of the line that has already been drawn.

3. The game goes on until one player draws a line that connects one end of the path to another. The winner is the player who does NOT close the path.

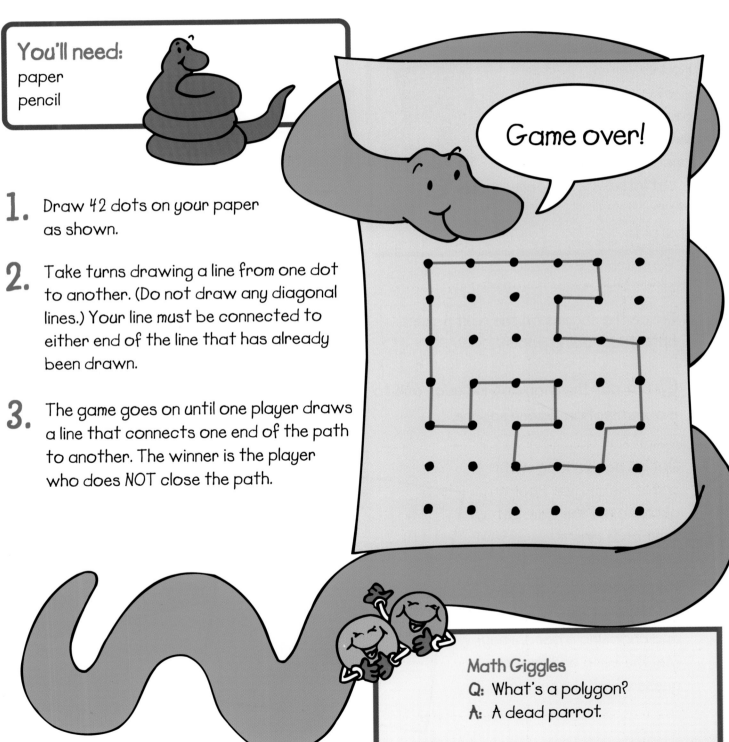

Game over!

Math Giggles
Q: What's a polygon?
A: A dead parrot.

Shape Flash Cards

2 players

Can you tell a shape by the way it feels?

You'll need:
tracing paper
pencil
scissors
glue
construction paper,
    cut into 5-inch squares
glitter
blindfold

5. The winner is the first player to make five correct guesses.

Tip: For more fun, make more cards with the other shapes you learn about in this section.

1. Trace the shapes on the next page onto the tracing paper.

2. (STOP) Cut out the shapes. Glue each one to a construction-paper square.

3. Outline each shape with a thin line of glue. Pour glitter over the glue. Let the cards dry.

4. To play the game, players take turns being blindfolded and choosing a card. They feel the card and try to guess which shape it is.

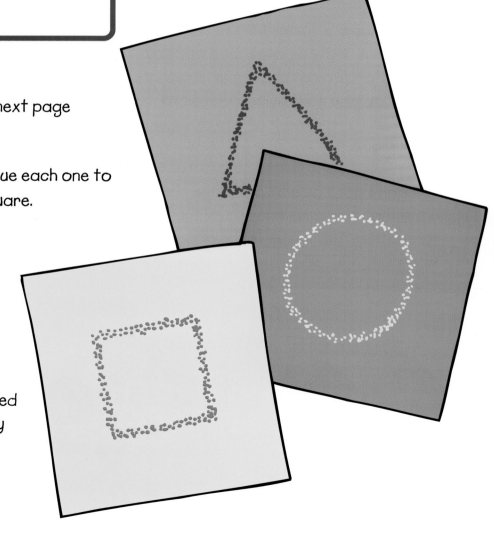

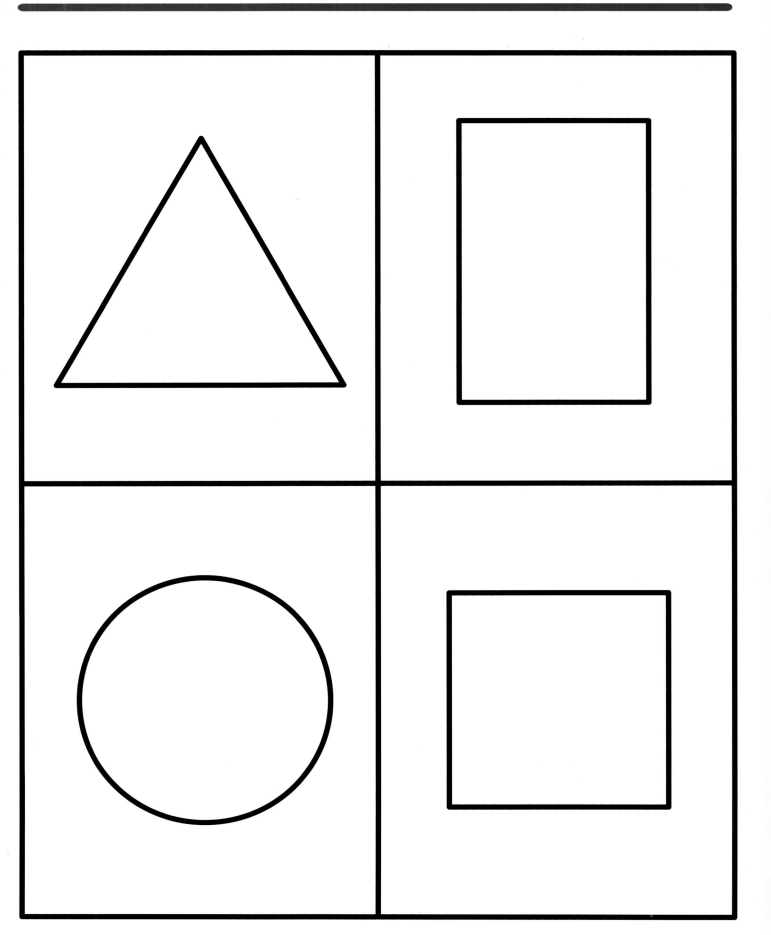

Dots

2 or 3 players

Build more boxes than the other players and you'll be the winner.

You'll need:
paper
pencil

1. Draw 100 dots on the paper, as shown.

2. Taking turns, draw a line between any two dots that are next to each other.

3. As you draw lines, try to make boxes. If you draw the final line to close a box, write your initials in that box. Then draw another line.

4. If a player closes two boxes at once when he draws a line, he still gets only one second turn.

5. The game continues until no more boxes can be closed. The winner is the player with the most boxes.

You can draw any number of dots on the paper—the more dots, the longer the game will be.

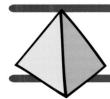

Making Shapes

Use these directions to make the shapes on pages 112 through 116.
The shapes on these pages are three-dimensional.
They have a length, a width, and a height.

You'll need:
tracing paper
pencil
scissors
glue
construction paper

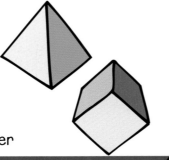

1. Trace one of the outlines on the following pages onto the tracing paper. **STOP** Cut out the design.

2. Glue the tracing-paper design onto a piece of construction paper. When it dries, cut the pattern out again.

3. Fold the paper on the dotted lines so that the tracing paper is on the inside.

4. Put a small amount of glue on each flap.

5. Press each flap against the edge of the shape that is next to the flap when it is folded. (It will be easy to tell where the flaps go.)

Try making a bunch of these shapes, and glue them together to make new and interesting designs. Try making mobiles, hats, or Christmas tree ornaments.

Tetrahedron Pattern

A tetrahedron (or a pyramid) is a shape with four equal triangular sides.

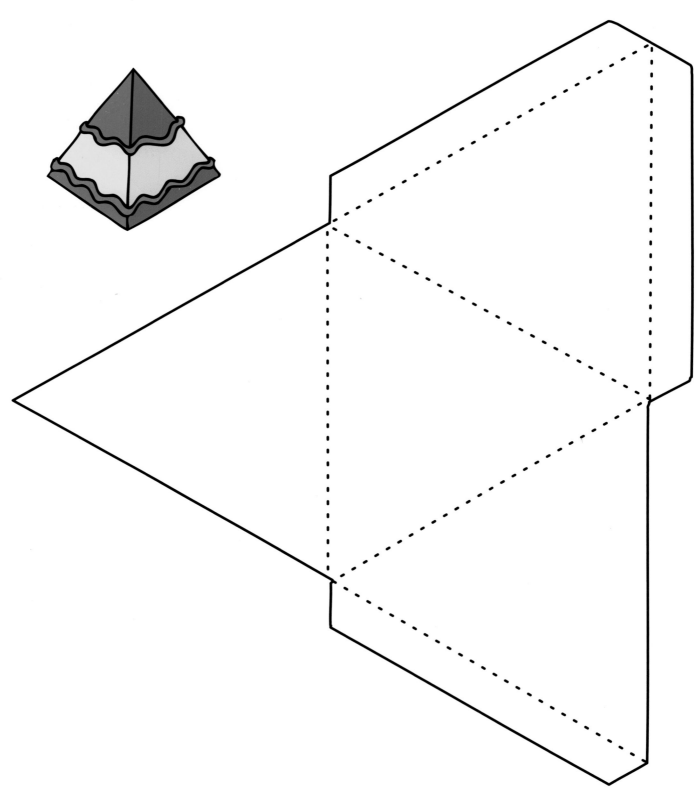

Cube Pattern

A cube has six equal square-shaped sides.

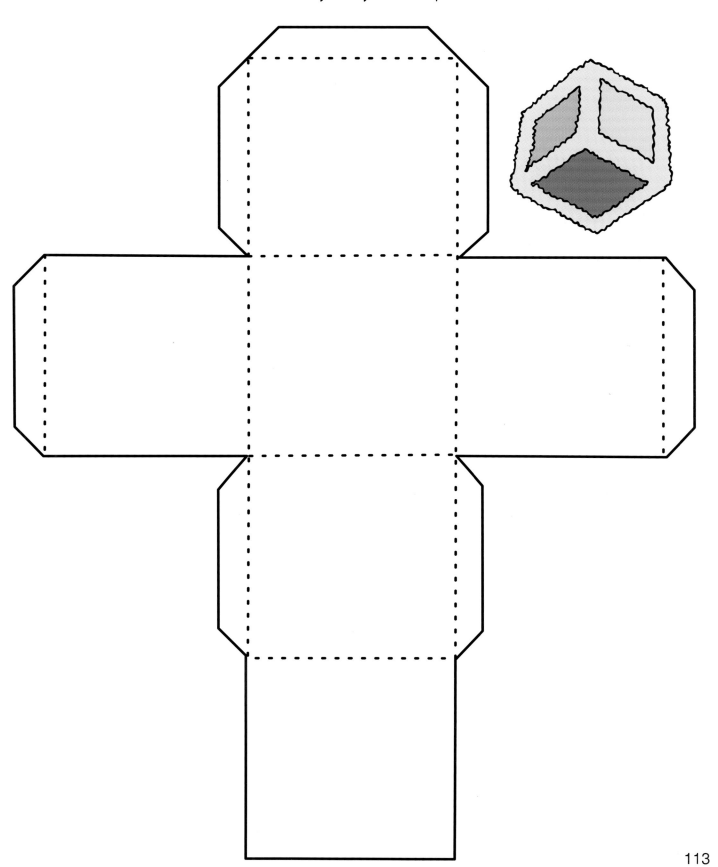

Octahedron Pattern

An octahedron is *diamond-shaped. It is made up of* eight equal triangles.

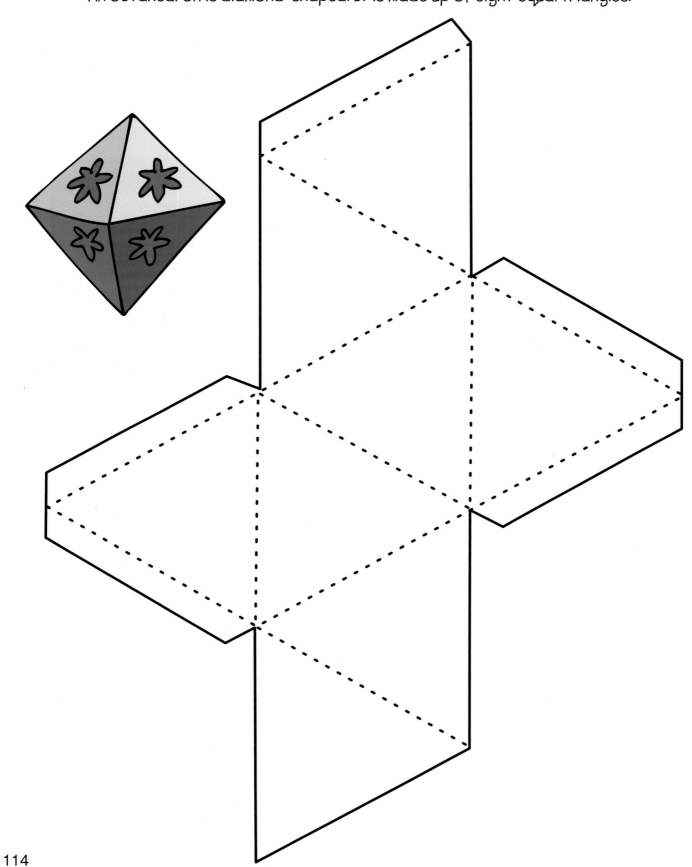

Dodecahedron Pattern

A dodecahedron has 12 equal pentagon-shaped sides.

To make this shape, fold and glue the sides in alphabetical order.

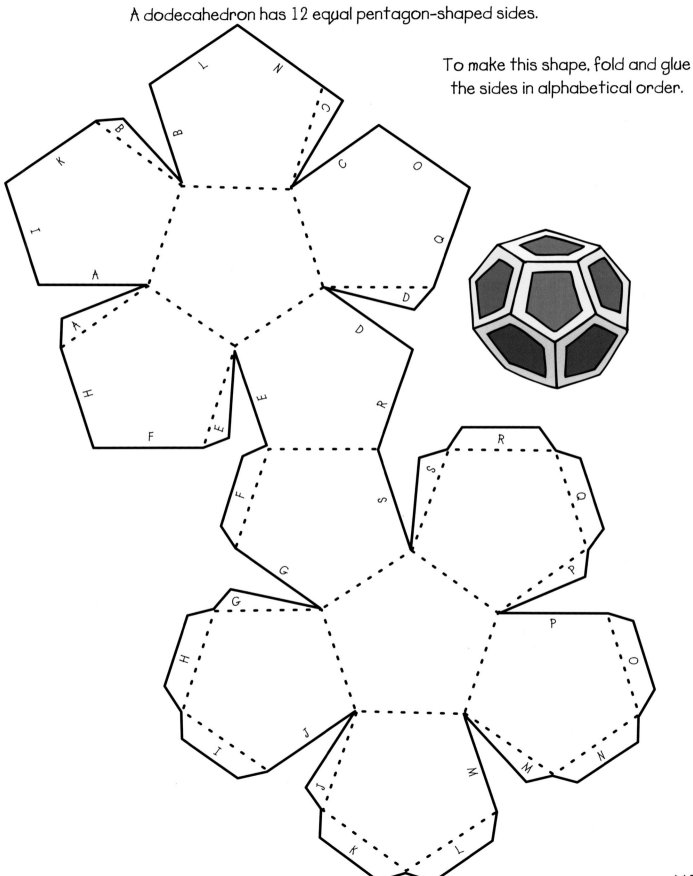

Icosahedron Pattern

An icosahedron has 20 equal triangle-shaped sides.

To make this shape, fold and glue the sides in alphabetical order.

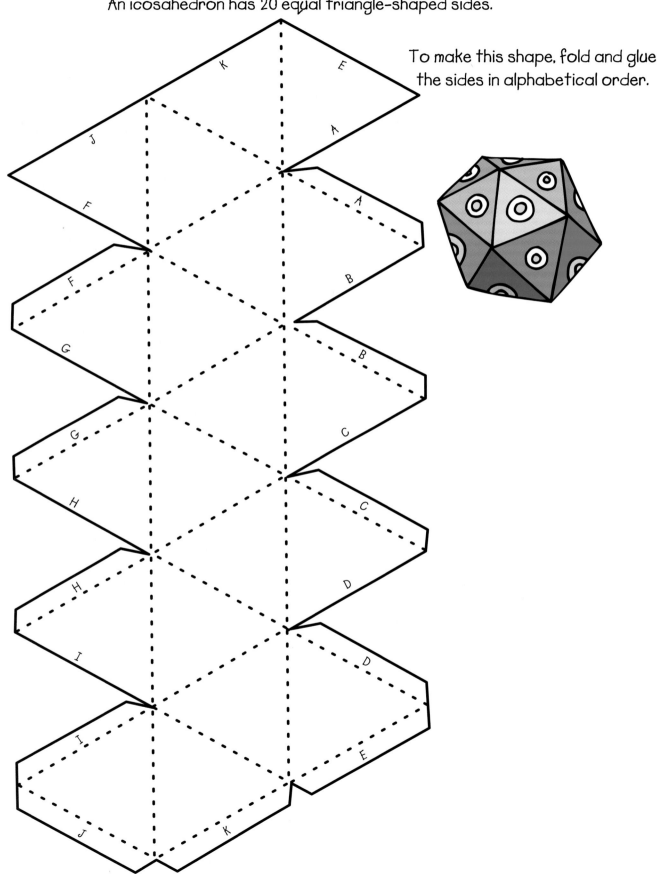

Money & Time

The nice thing about money and time is they get easier to understand as you learn how to count them. Once you know the basics, they don't change. For the rest of your life, counting money and telling time will be done exactly the same way. There aren't more challenging ways that no one has told you about yet. So get busy practicing, and soon you'll be able to count money and time as well as grown-ups can.

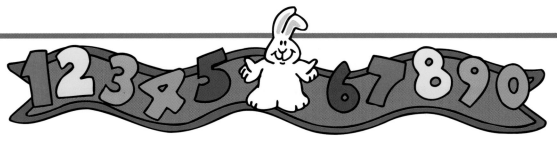

Adding It Up—Money

Here is what the money from the United States looks like:

Quarter

Penny

Five-Dollar Bill

Half-Dollar

One-Dollar Bill

Twenty-Dollar Bill

Ten-Dollar Bill

Nickel

Dime

One Hundred-Dollar Bill

Shopping Spree

2 or more players
Spend your money wisely.

You'll need:
several catalogs
pencils
paper
calculator

1. Each player gets a piece of paper and a pencil. Put the catalogs in the middle of the table.

2. Pretend you are buying presents for your family. You have $50 to spend. Look through the catalogs. As you find items you'd like to "buy," write down what they are and how much they cost. Keep track of how much you are spending as you go along. (Do not use the calculator.)

3. Time yourselves. Allow only ten minutes to do your shopping.

4. The winner is the player who spends the amount closest to $50 without going over $50. Use the calculator to check your work.

Other ways to play:
See who can buy the most items with $50. Or change the amount of money you can spend. Or limit the kind of item you can buy—maybe you can buy only toys, or only clothes, or only socks.

Party Budget

Can you throw a great party and stay within your budget?

You'll need:
pencil
paper
calculator

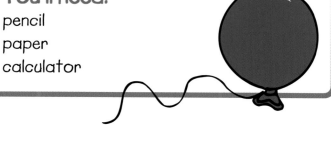

1. Pretend you are throwing a party, and Mom and Dad will let you spend $20. Make a list of what you will need for the party. Guess how much each thing will cost.

2. Ask a grown-up to take you to the grocery store. Look at the prices of the things you have on your list. Write them down. Add them up. Did you have enough money?

Other ways to play:
You can make this a two-player game. Both of you make up a list and go to the store. The person who is closest to the $20, whether under or over, is the winner.

Dinner Out

Is your favorite restaurant the best buy?

You'll need:
menus from some local restaurants
pencil
paper
calculator

2 burgers for me, 2 burgers for Mom, 2 burgers for Sally, 2 burgers for Jason, and 6 burgers. . .

1. Pretend that you are taking your family out to dinner. Look through some menus. For each menu, write down what each family member would order and what it would probably cost. About how much money do you need to take your family out to dinner? Which restaurant would cost the most money? Which would cost the least? How could you save some money at the restaurant?

Other ways to play:
To play with another person, set a price limit for your meal, and decide how many people will be coming. Looking at a menu, write down the different dishes you would order. The person who can order the most food for everyone at the table without going over the price limit is the winner.

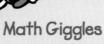

Math Giggles
Q: Why is a nickel smarter than a penny?
A: Because a nickel has more sense (cents).

Magnificent Money Toss

2 or more players

Can you toss the most money into the bowl?

You'll need:

2 small paper bowls
masking tape
pennies, nickels, dimes, quarters
pencil
paper

1. Fold a piece of masking tape in a loop and place it on the bottom of one bowl. Set the bowl on the floor, so it sticks.

2. Take about six steps from the bowl, and put a strip of masking tape on the floor.

3. Place the second bowl next to the masking tape strip. Place the coins inside the bowl.

4. Players take turns tossing coins into the empty bowl. On each turn, you have five chances to throw, and you can throw any coin you want. You must throw one coin at a time.

5. When a player has tossed his five coins, count the amount of change in the bowl. Write that number under the player's name on the score sheet. Put the coins back in the coin bowl and let the next player toss.

Score Sheet		
John	Liz	Terry
$.60	$.75	$.49
$.73		

6. At the end of the game, add up the amounts. The winner is the player who tosses the biggest amount of money into the bowl.

123

Adding It Up—
Who Invented Money?

All over the world, people use all different kinds of money. But there was a time when there was no money at all—at least not the paper bills and coins that you have in your pocket.

Long ago, people would *barter*. When you barter, you give someone a good or service, and they give you one back. Let's say you want to barter with your friend so she will give you a piece of bubble gum. You might give her a piece of hard candy so she will give you the gum. Bartering is like trading.

But bartering can take a lot of time. If you want something from someone, but you don't have anything that person wants to trade for, you must first trade with another person to get something the first person wants. Confusing, huh?

So people started wondering what kinds of currency they could use. *Currency* means "something that is used to buy a good or service." People used beads, stones, shells, cocoa beans, and other small items for money. They would also use gold, silver, and copper, which became very popular.

The first coins were probably made in a country called Lydia, which is now part of Turkey. In the 600s B.C., they made small bean-shaped bits of a gold and silver mixture. India and China also were among the first countries to use coins. And the Chinese were using paper money starting in the A.D. 600s.

Most of the coins we use today in the United States are made in Denver and Philadelphia. When a coin is made, it is *minted*. It is a law that U.S. all coins must have the year they were minted, the word "Liberty," and the Latin motto "E Pluribus Unum" (which means "out of many, one") somewhere on each coin.

The government is in charge of printing and coining money. But they don't make money all day, every day. If too much money is made, it won't be worth anything. So government officials take care that there is only a certain amount of money in circulation.

Try this:
• Try to collect coins stamped with the year you were born. How much money can you save?
• Look carefully at a one-dollar bill. What kinds of markings does it have?
• Try to figure out what all the words and numbers stand for on a dollar bill.
• Borrow a book from the library on how money is made.

ArithmeTRICK: More Nifty Nines

Here are a couple of interesting facts about 9.

You'll need:
paper
pencil
calculator

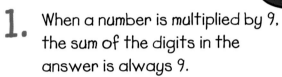

1. When a number is multiplied by 9, the sum of the digits in the answer is always 9.

   $9 \times 2 = 18 \rightarrow 1 + 8 = 9$

   $9 \times 6 = 54 \rightarrow 5 + 4 = 9$

   $9 \times 271 = 2439 \rightarrow 2 + 4 + 3 + 9 = 18 \rightarrow 1 + 8 = 9$

2. To multiply any number by 9:
   - Add 0 to that number.

     9×34567

     345670
   - Subtract the original number.

     $345670 - 34567$
   - And that's the answer:

     9×34567 or

     $345670 - 34567 = 311103$

3. If any number can be evenly divided by 9, the digits of that number will add up to 9:

   $27639 \div 9 = 3071$

   $2 + 7 + 6 + 3 + 9 = 27$ and $2 + 7 = 9$

Your Busy Schedule

*Help your family keep track of your busy life,
and post this schedule on your bedroom door.*

You'll need:
paper
crayons

1. Write down the things you do during the day—wake up, leave for school, eat lunch, get out of school, get home from baseball practice, do your homework, eat dinner, watch your favorite television show, go to bed, or anything else you do.

2. Write down what time you do each thing, next to each activity.

3. Next to each written time, draw a clock that shows that time.

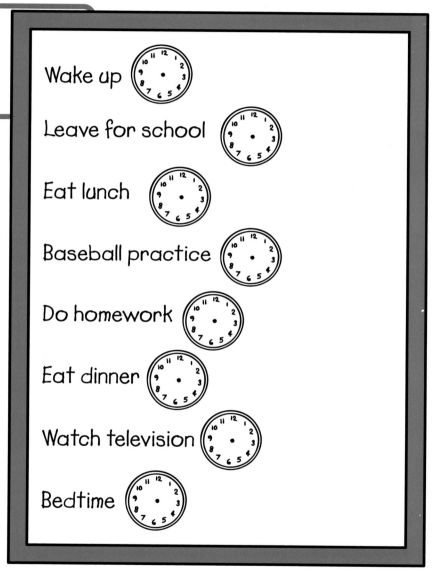

Wake up

Leave for school

Eat lunch

Baseball practice

Do homework

Eat dinner

Watch television

Bedtime

Math Giggles
Q: Why is a calendar sad?
A: Its days are numbered.

The Race for Time

2 players
How well do you tell time?

You'll need:
old clock with hands you can move
pencil
paper

1. Set the hands of the clock to any time you want. Show the clock to the other player. Ask her what time it is.

2. If she knows the correct time, she gets a point. If she doesn't, you get a point.

3. Then it is the other player's turn to set the clock.

4. The player with the most points wins.

5. You can also make the game more challenging by setting a time and then asking questions like:
   - What time will it be in three hours?
   - What time was it 1 hour and 15 minutes ago?
   - How long ago did we get out of school?

Tip: If you play with a grown-up, or someone who tells time really well, you can change the rules a bit. When the other player makes his guess about what time the clock shows, he can tell the truth, or he can make something up. It is up to you to know whether he is right or wrong.

If he says the wrong time and you catch him, you get the point. If you don't catch the mistake, he gets the point. If he says the right time and you think he's wrong, he also gets the point. No one gets the point if he says the right time and you agree with him. When it is your turn to guess, points work the same way as in the original game: If you answer correctly, you get the point, and if you are wrong, the other player gets the point.

Seconds Tick Away

3 players
How much can you cram into a minute?

You'll need:
watch or clock with a second hand
pencil
paper
bowl

1. Tear the paper into small strips. On each strip write a question about something that must be done in a certain amount of time. For example:
  - How long can you hold your breath?
  - How many times can you hop up and down on one foot in 30 seconds?
  - How long can you stand on one foot?
  - How long can you keep yourself from blinking?
  - How many times can you rub your tummy in 15 seconds?
  - How many times can you clap your hands in 15 seconds?
  - How many times can you write your name in one minute?

2. Put the slips of paper in the bowl. Take turns drawing a slip of paper from the bowl. Do what it says. One player watches the clock. The other player counts how many times you do something, if necessary.

3. There are two ways to score: If you had to see how many times you could do something in a certain amount of time, your score is the number of times you did it. If you had to see how long you could do something, your score is that time, in seconds.

4. The player with the most points wins.

ArithmeTRICK: Ages & Ages I

You'll need:
paper
pencil
calculator

Here's a way to figure out someone's age.

1. Ask a friend to secretly multiply his age by 3 .

   8 x 3 = 24

2. Have him secretly add 6 to the answer.

   24 + 6 = 30

3. Next tell him to divide that answer by 3 and to tell you the answer.

   30 ÷ 3 = 10

4. He will laugh because he knows 10 is not his age.

5. Now you secretly subtract 2 from the number he told you.

   10 – 2 = 8

   That is your friend's real age.

ArithmeTRICK: Ages & Ages II

You'll need:
paper
pencil
calculator

Here's another crafty way to figure out someone's age.

1. Write down the year you were born.
1970

2. Double it.
1970 + 1970 = 3940

3. Add 5 to that answer.
3940 + 5 = 3945

4. Multiply that answer by 50.
3945 x 50 = 197250

5. Add your age.
197250 + 26 = 197276

6. Add 365.
197276 + 365 = 197641

7. Subtract 615.
197641 − 615 = 197026

The first four numbers are the year you were born. The last two numbers are your age.

Any Minute Now

Make it easier to learn how to tell time.

You'll need:
clock on a wall
construction paper
pencil
scissors
tape

1. On the construction paper, draw a design that you like. It can be a star, a dinosaur, a baseball, a dog, or anything.

2. **STOP** Make 12 of these designs, and cut them out.

3. Number each design with one of the numbers shown on a star above.

4. Ask a grown-up to tape your numbered designs around the wall clock, in the order they are arranged above.

5. Use these numbers when you are practicing how to tell time.

Math Giggles
Q: Two fathers and two sons have three dollars. Each one takes a dollar. How is that possible?
A: There were only three people: a grandfather, a father, and a son.

Sundial

Make your own version of an ancient timekeeper.

You'll need:

small ball of clay
small flowerpot
chopstick
ruler
marker
watch

1. Press the clay into the bottom of the flowerpot. Push one end of the chopstick into the clay. About three inches of the chopstick should stick up above the top of the pot.

2. When the sun is rising, put the flowerpot outside in a sunny spot. Make a mark on the rim of the flowerpot where the chopstick makes a shadow. Write what time it is next to this mark.

3. For the rest of the day, mark the spot where the shadow hits the edge of the pot at each hour until the sun sets (at 7:00 A.M., 8:00 A.M., 9:00 A.M., etc.). Be sure to write the time next to each mark.

4. Now you have a sundial! Leave the pot in the same place, and you will be able to tell the approximate time of day by using the sun.

Adding It Up—"Clock-wise"

Electric clocks were first made in 1840. *Alarm clocks* came along in 1847. The *watch* you wear on your arm wasn't invented until 1907. So how did people know what time it was before then?

For thousands of years, people have been thinking up ways to keep track of the time.

In ancient times, many people used the *hourglass*. An hourglass is filled with sand. You turn it over and when all the sand pours from one side to the other, a certain amount of time has passed. The Egyptians, the Greeks, and the Chinese (who probably invented it) all used the hourglass. But it's really hard to wear an hourglass on your wrist!

Ancient people also used *sundials*. A sundial uses a stick that makes a shadow on the ground. As the shadow moves around, people can tell what time it is.

A *waterclock* was also used in ancient times. It was a bucket filled with water that had marks drawn on the side. A small hole was made in the bottom so the water could leak out. As it leaked, the water in the bucket would go down. As it went down, people could tell how much time had passed.

People also told time with a candle. Marks were made on a candle and when the candle burned down to a mark, an hour had passed.

Starting in the late 10th century, inventors began making clocks that worked with springs, weights, and pendulums. Many required keys or had to be wound up. *Pendulum clocks* (the clocks with the big arms that swing back and forth) were invented in 1654.

The clocks and watches you use today are usually *quartz clocks*. A quartz clock has a quartz crystal inside that vibrates back and forth. The vibrations are caused by a small battery in the clock.

Try this:

- Make a waterclock. Fill a paper cup and take it outside. Use a needle to poke a small hole in the bottom of the cup. Notice the time as soon as you poke the hole. Notice the time when the cup is empty. Now you know how long it takes the cup to empty, and you can use it to tell time.
- Look for different kinds of clocks around your house. You may find an hourglass, a sundial, a pendulum clock, or a quartz clock.
- Try making a candle clock. Measure a candle from top to bottom. With a grown-up's help, light the candle. Let the candle burn for 15 minutes. Blow it out and let it cool. Now measure the candle again. With that measurement, figure out how far apart you would make the hour marks on a candle clock.

Calculators

Calculators are an easy way to check your work. And sometimes, they are a necessary shortcut to finding the answer. That's why this book includes a bunch of fun games to try with your calculator. But don't think you can get away with learning about math by using a calculator. To use your calculator the right way, you still need to understand how math works.

Seven Signs

2 players
Can you reach 7 before your opponent does?

You'll need:
calculator

1. Press the CLEAR button (CE/C button) on the calculator. Be sure the calculator display reads "0."

2. Take turns adding 1 or 2 to the calculated sum.

3. The first player to reach 7 without going over is the winner.

Math Giggles
Q: When something goes wrong, what can you always count on?
A: Your fingers.

ArithmeTRICK: Calculator Riddles

Use your calculator to find the answers.

You'll need:
calculator

1. What animal lays golden eggs?
- Start with 1000 animals.
- Multiply by 30 because they laid 30 eggs each.
- Subtract 20,000 because they stepped on that many eggs.
- Multiply by 3 because the farmer fed the animals three eggs a day.
- Add 6006 because that's how many visitors took pictures of the animals.
- Subtract 1000 because the visitors bought 1000 eggs.
- Turn your calculator upside down to read the answer.

2. What part of your body do you stand on?
- Start with 6000 roller coaster seats.
- Subtract 1000 because that many people got on.
- Add 37 because only 37 people were brave enough to ride—everybody else got off.
- Multiply by 2 because the ride cost $2.00.
- Subtract 5037 pieces of popcorn that flew up in the air.
- Add 600 because 600 other people watched the popcorn fall.
- Turn your calculator upside down for the answer.

Answers: 1. goose 2. legs

Countdown 11

2 players
Can you be the first to reach 0?

You'll need:
calculator

1. Press the CLEAR button on the calculator. Make sure the display reads "0."

2. Enter 11 into the calculator.

3. Take turns subtracting 1 or 2.

4. The winner is the first person to reach 0.

2 players

Try this electronic version of a popular card game.

You'll need:
calculator

1. Press the CLEAR button on the calculator. Be sure the display reads "0."

2. Take turns entering either 1, 2, 3, or 4.

3. The first player to reach 21 without going over is the winner.

Math Giggles

Q: What's the difference between 100 and 1000?

A: Nothing (a zero).

Run From 101

2 or more players
Which number should you choose?

You'll need:
calculator

Press CLEAR. Be sure your calculator display reads "0."

101 into the calculator.

turns subtracting 1, 2, 3, 4, 5, 6, 7, 8, 9 from the number. The player who makes the display read "0" wins.

Try starting at 0 and adding the numbers to reach 101 without going over it.

ArithmeTRICK: Calculator Code

You'll need:
calculator

Punch these numbers into your calculator. Turn the calculator upside down to find the hidden words.

7718	7334
7714	818
7738	77345
8078	345
40	3045
3704	7735

Answers: bill, hill, bell, blob, oh, hole, heel, bib, shell, she, shoe, sell

3001 Math Odyssey

2 or more players
You won't know who is winning until the very end.

You'll need:
calculator

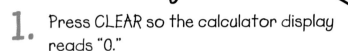

1. Press CLEAR so the calculator display reads "0."

2. Enter the number 3001 into the calculator.

3. Taking turns, subtract any number from 1–99. Press the equal sign after you punch in the subtraction sign and number each time. The person who reaches 0 is the winner.

Math Giggles
Q: Which would you prefer—an old $10 bill or a new one?
A: An old $10 bill is better than a new $1 bill.

Reason & Strategy

A great way to practice the thinking and logic skills you need for math is to play games that use reasoning and strategy. That means you need to think and plan ahead in order to win. And thinking and reasoning can be fun! Match your wits against your friends and family, and see who comes out ahead.

Tapatan

2 players

This is a version of tic-tac-toe.

You'll need:

piece of white paper
2 different-colored sheets of construction paper
ruler
black marker
scissors

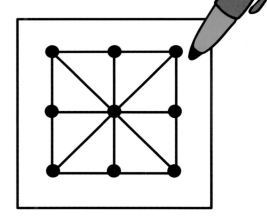

1. On the white paper, use the ruler and marker to draw a gameboard like the one below.

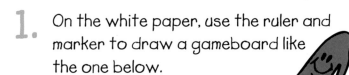

2. 🛑 Using the construction paper, cut out six small circles, three of one color and three of the other.

3. Place the board on the table between both players. Each player gets three circles of the same color.

4. To begin, take turns putting one circle on one of the points on the board until all the cards are placed.

5. Then, take turns sliding your circles around, trying to get your three in a straight line.

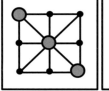

6. To move your circle, you can move only one point over and the point you are moving to must be free. You can't jump over another circle. There can be only one circle on each point.

7. The winner is the first player to get his three circles in a row. There may not be a winner at every game.

145

Mancala

2 players

This is a version of an old African stone game.

You'll need:

1 egg carton
markers or paint/paintbrush
2 small paper plates
48 colored beads or small pebbles

1. Decorate the egg carton with markers or paint, if you like. If you want to store the playing pieces in the carton, leave the top on. If you don't want to, cut the lid off.

2. Set the egg carton on the table between both players, so one long side of the egg carton is facing each player. Place a paper plate next to each end of the carton. Put four beads or pebbles in each cup of the egg carton.

3. Players take turns. When you go, pick up the beads in any one of the cups on your side of the board. Moving in a clockwise direction, place one bead in each of the following cups until there are no beads left in your hand. It is okay to drop beads in the cups on the other side of the board. The two plates are part of the board also. So as you move down the line, don't forget to drop one in the plate as you pass it.

4. If you put the last bead in your hand in one of the paper plates, you get to go again. The beads on the plates are out of play. You cannot pick them up and drop them into cups. If you do not drop your last bead on a plate when it is your turn, it is the next player's turn. You must drop one bead in each cup, in order.

5. The player who gets rid of all the beads on his side of the board first is the winner.

ArithmeTRICK: Which Card?

You'll need:
paper
pencil
deck of cards

1. Ask a grown-up to pick any card from the deck. Tell him to write down the number and suit of the card on a piece of paper. (The suit is the "decoration" on the card—clubs, spades, hearts, or diamonds.) For this trick, an ace is 1, a jack is 11, a queen is 12, and a king is 13. For example, let's say your helper picks the 10 of diamonds.

2. Tell your helper to double the number on the card.

$$\begin{array}{r} 10 \\ + 10 \\ \hline 20 \end{array}$$

3. Add 2 to that answer.

$$\begin{array}{r} 20 \\ + 2 \\ \hline 22 \end{array}$$

4. Multiply that answer by 5.

$$\begin{array}{r} 22 \\ \times 5 \\ \hline 110 \end{array}$$

5. Add the correct suit number to that answer (see below).

$$\begin{array}{r} 110 \\ + 2 \\ \hline 112 \end{array}$$

110 + 2 (for diamonds) = 112
Ask the grown-up what his final answer is.

6. Now you subtract 10 from that answer.

$$\begin{array}{r} 112 \\ - 10 \\ \hline 102 \end{array}$$

7. The one or two numbers on the left tell you the number of the card, and the number on the right tells you the suit number (according to the chart). 102=10 of diamonds

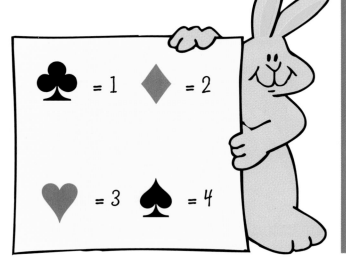

♣ = 1   ♦ = 2

♥ = 3   ♠ = 4

Odd One Out

2 players
Who will get stuck with the odd one out?

You'll need:
12 beans
1 penny

1. Place the beans and the penny on the floor between you.

2. Take turns removing one or two beans.

3. The person who takes the penny is the loser.

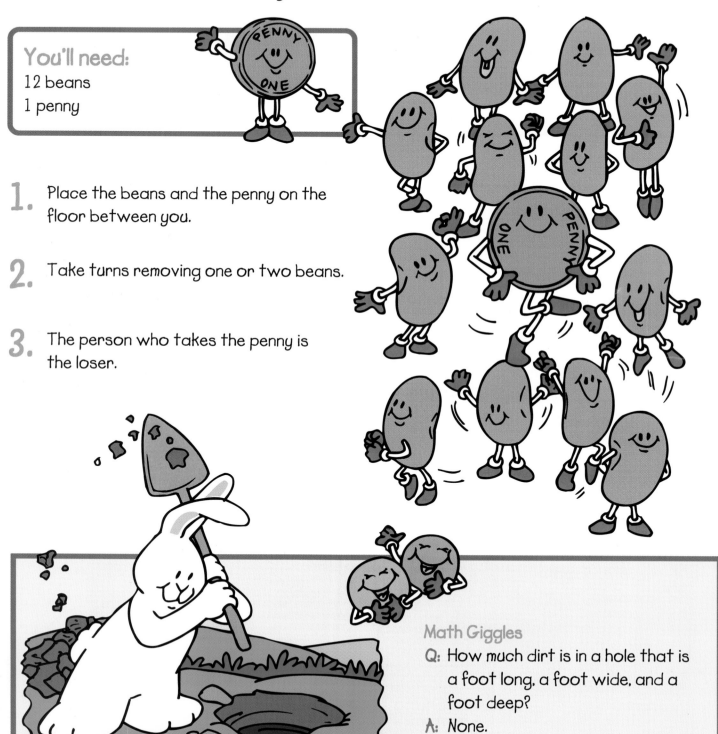

Math Giggles
Q: How much dirt is in a hole that is a foot long, a foot wide, and a foot deep?
A: None.

148

Say 25

2 or more players
This is a great game for class field trips or family vacations!

You'll need: nothing!

25!

1. Take turns counting off one or two numbers.

2. The first player to reach 25 is the winner.

1 player
Can you figure out this tricky puzzle?

You'll need:
5 playing cards—an ace, a 2, a 3, a 4, and a 5

1. Lay out the cards as shown below.

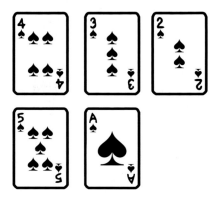

2. The object of the puzzle is to arrange the cards in order (the ace is 1). But to do it, you can only slide a card into an adjoining empty space. For example, you could move the 2 down or the 2 over. Continue sliding until you have the cards in order (ace, 2, 3 on top and 4, 5 on the bottom).

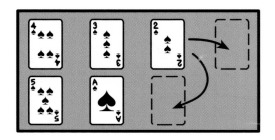

3. If you need the quickest solution, see page 152.

Answers to Tangram Puzzles on page 101.

Answers to Moving Cards on page 150.

1. Move the 2 to the right.
2. Move the 3 to the right.
3. Move the 4 down.
4. Move the ace to the left.
5. Move the 5 to the left.
6. Move the 2 up.
7. Move the 3 to the right.
8. Move the 5 down.
9. Move the 2 to the left.
10. Move the 3 up.

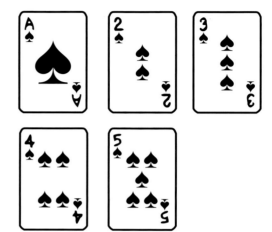

Answer to Toothpick Magic on page 42.

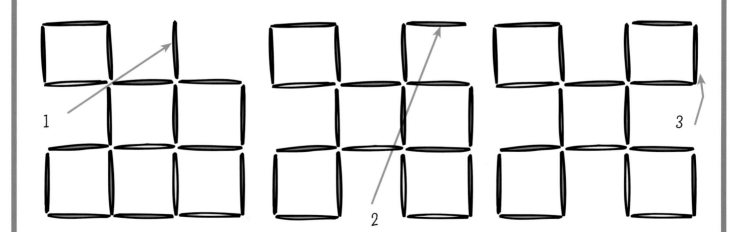

Glossary

Arithmetic
Part of mathematics in which you study numbers and adding, subtracting, multiplying, and dividing.

Circle
A curved line that closes. Every point on the line is the same distance from the center.

Cube
A three-dimensional figure that looks like a box. It has six faces that are all squares and all the same size.

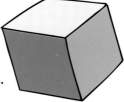

Diagonal
A line from one corner to the opposite corner (not the corner next to it).

Digit
One of the numerals in a number. In the number 15, the digits are 1 and 5.

Dodecahedron
A figure with 12 faces that is three-dimensional.

Even Number
A number that can be divided evenly by two.

2, 4, 6, 8, 10, 12, 14, 16, 18, 20, ...

Glossary

Fraction
A number that expresses part of a whole.

1/2, 1/4, 1/8, 2/3, 3/4

Hexagon
A flat figure with six sides.

Hexahedron
A six-faced figure that is three-dimensional.

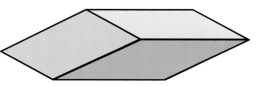

Icosahedron
A figure with 20 faces that is three-dimensional.

Infinity
Something with no beginning and no end. Numbers go on to infinity because you can always add one to a number and get a bigger number.

Integer
A whole numbr, like 1, 2, 3, 4, etc.

Multiples
All the numbers created when you multiply a numeral with another numeral are multiples of that numeral. For example,

2 x 3 = 6, 2 x 4 = 8, and 2 x 5 = 10.

That means 6, 8, and 10 are multiples of 2.

Glossary

Number
A symbol that stands for a certain amount.

Numeral
A symbol for a digit.

Octagon
A flat figure with eight sides.

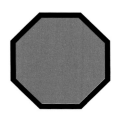

Octahedron
A figure with eight faces that is three-dimensional.

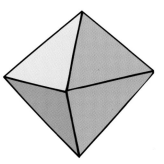

Odd Number
A number that cannot be divided evenly by two.

1, 3, 5, 7, 9, 11, 13, 15, 17, 19, ...

Parallel
When two lines are going in the same direction and are always the same distance apart.

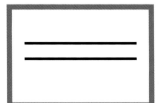

Pentagon
A flat figure with five sides.

Percent
Part of one whole.

Place Value
The value of a digit, depending on where it is located in a number. For example, in the number 537, there are five hundreds, three tens, and seven ones.

Glossary

Prime Number

A number that can only be divided evenly by itself and one. One is not a prime number.

Square

A flat figure with four equal sides.

Tetrahedron

A figure with four faces that is three-dimensional.

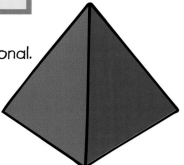

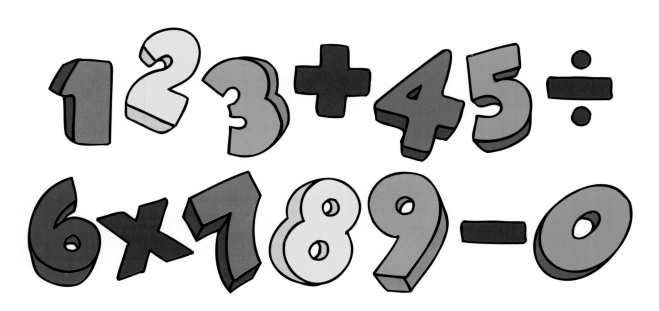

INDEX

INDEX

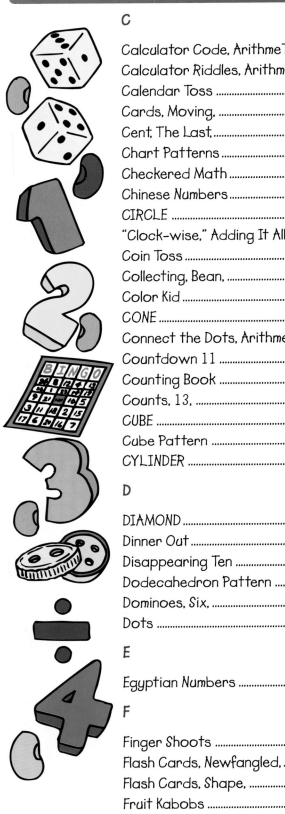

INDEX

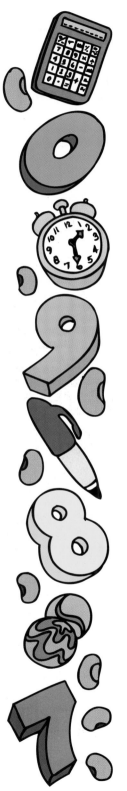

INDEX